Currier & Ives Four Seasons Cookbook

Currier & Ives Four Seasons Cookbook

MALLARD PRESS
An Imprint of BDD Promotional Book Company, Inc.
666 Fifth Avenue
New York, New York 10103

Photographic material courtesy of the Museum of the City of New York.
Photographs on pages 10, 18, 19, 34, 35, 38, 54, 58, 66, 82, 83, 87, 98, 99, 102, 106, 107, 114, 115 and cover, courtesy of The Harry T. Peters Collection, the Museum of the City of New York.

Created and manufactured by arrangement with Ottenheimer Publishers, Inc.

Copyright © 1990 Ottenheimer Publishers, Inc.

"Mallard Press and its accompanying design and logo are trademarks of BDD Promotional Book Company, Inc."

First published in the United States of America in 1990 by The Mallard Press.

Printed in Hong Kong

Contents

American Country Life—May Morning

Spring

SOUPS & APPETIZERS

Mexican Meat Balls

4 DOZEN MEAT BALLS

1 pound ground beef
1/2 green pepper, finely chopped
1 garlic clove
1 onion, grated
1 egg yolk
Salt and pepper, to taste
1 tablespoon capers
1 tablespoon olives, chopped
1/2 cup bread crumbs
2 tablespoons vinegar
1 tablespoon vegetable oil
Sauce:
1/2 cup consommé
1/2 cup onion, chopped
1 6-ounce can tomato paste
2 slices bacon, chopped

Mix ground beef with other ingredients. Roll into balls. Sauté quickly in oil.

Combine sauce ingredients in saucepan. Add meatballs to sauce. Be sure meatballs are covered with sauce ingredients. Cover and simmer for 30 minutes.

Crab Meat Canapés

20 CANAPÉS

1/2 pound crab meat, cartilage removed
1 cup mayonnaise
2 egg whites, beaten
1/2 teaspoon salt
1 1/2 teaspoons pepper
Pinch of mace
10 slices white bread

Pre-heat broiler.

Mix together crab meat, mayonnaise, egg whites, salt, pepper, and mace. Cut bread slices into canapé shapes and toast briefly on one side. Spread with crab mixture on untoasted side. Sprinkle with paprika.
Broil several minutes until mixture bubbles.

Russian Borscht

6 SERVINGS

7 to 8 cups chicken consommé
1 cup uncooked beets, julienned
2 1/2 cups uncooked beets, finely chopped
1 cup carrots, chopped
1 cup onions, chopped
1 tablespoon red wine vinegar
Salt, to taste
2 egg yolks
1 tablespoon sugar
1 1/2 cups sour cream
2 tablespoons fresh lemon juice
1 cucumber, diced
1/4 cup minced fresh dill

Pour consommé into large soup kettle, reserving 1 cup. Place 1 cup consommé and julienned beets in a small saucepan and simmer, covered, for approximately 10 minutes. Strain mixture into soup kettle. Reserve julienned beets.

Bring consommé to boiling point. Add chopped uncooked beets, carrots, and onions; stir in vinegar and salt. Cook, covered, over medium heat for 15 to 20 minutes or until vegetables are soft. Strain into bowl, discard vegetables and chill.

In soup tureen, beat together egg yolks, sugar, sour cream, and lemon juice; blend until smooth. Gradually whisk in chilled broth to make smooth mixture. If mixture becomes lumpy, strain again. Chill for 15 to 20 minutes.

To serve, add cucumber, reserved julienned beets and sprinkle with dill.

Chopped Liver

6 SERVINGS

1 pound calves liver
1 large onion, coarsely chopped
2 hard-boiled eggs, sieved
Salt and pepper, to taste
2 tablespoons boiling water

Pre-heat broiler.

Broil liver, then cut up in small pieces. Add coarsely chopped onion, eggs, salt, and pepper. Chop finely, adding 2 tablespoons boiling water while chopping. Form into a preferred shape and serve with crackers.

Cheese Puffs

12 PUFFS

1/4 cup Swiss cheese, grated
2 egg whites
Cracker crumbs, to coat
Oil, to sauté

Mix together grated Swiss cheese and egg whites. Shape into tiny balls and roll in fine cracker crumbs. Sauté quickly in hot oil and serve immediately.

Spinach Soup

4 TO 6 SERVINGS

2 pounds fresh spinach
8 cups chicken stock
3 tablespoons butter
2 tablespoons flour
1 teaspoon salt
Dash of freshly ground black pepper
1/8 teaspoon nutmeg
Hard-boiled egg, sliced, to garnish

Wash spinach thoroughly and drain. Chop coarsely. Bring chicken stock to a boil in 4-quart soup pot and add spinach. Simmer uncovered for approximately 8 minutes. Strain spinach, pressing with a spoon to remove most of liquid. If desired, chop cooked spinach again.

Melt butter in same 4-quart soup pot, then remove from heat. Whisk in flour. Add liquid stock, 1 cup at a time, stirring constantly. Return to heat and bring to a boil. Add spinach, salt, pepper, and nutmeg. Simmer for approximately 5 minutes to thicken soup. To serve, garnish with hard-boiled egg slices.

Lentil Soup

6 SERVINGS

Ham or beef bone
1 pound lentils
12 cups chicken stock
2 large onions, chopped
½ cup carrots, grated
4 tablespoons butter
1 teaspoon thyme

Put bone, lentils, and stock into deep pot. Bring to boil and simmer for 1 hour and 30 minutes. Remove bone.

In frying pan, sauté onions and carrots in butter until onions are transparent, do not brown. Add onions and carrots to lentils with thyme, and simmer 30 minutes longer.

Cream of Scallop Soup

8 SERVINGS

1 pound fresh scallops
5 cups chicken broth
1 cup dry white wine
4 tablespoons butter
1 tablespoon curry powder
2 cups heavy cream
3 egg yolks
Paprika, to garnish

Wash scallops under cold water; drain well. Combine chicken broth and white wine in stainless steel or enamel pot and bring to a boil. Add scallops, simmer for 2 minutes, then remove with slotted spoon.

Melt butter with curry powder in frying pan and sauté for 1 minute. Add scallops and sauté for 4 minutes.

Place scallops, with any remaining butter, into food processor, using steel blade. Start the motor and slowly feed cream through processor tube. Blend until reduced to smooth puree. Whisk puree into broth. If soup is to be eaten later, refrigerate, but do not cover.

Before serving, bring soup to a boil. Beat egg yolks. Whisk about 1½ cups of boiling soup in a thin stream into beaten egg yolks. Whisk egg-soup mixture into remaining soup, over low heat. Stir briskly for 1 minute and turn off heat. Do not let soup boil once egg mixture has been added.

Serve in hot bowls, garnished with sprinkling of paprika.

Horseradish Ham Rolls

8 ROLLS

½ cup heavy cream
1 teaspoon sugar
2 tablespoons prepared horseradish
½ cup macaroni, cooked
8 slices cooked ham
¼ cup Swiss cheese, shredded

Whip heavy cream until stiff. Add sugar and horseradish. Gently fold in cooked macaroni. Spread mixture on ham slices and roll up.

Arrange on serving platter and sprinkle ham rolls with shredded cheese.

Watercress Soup

4 SERVINGS

2 bunches watercress
5 tablespoons butter or margarine
4 cups milk
1½ cups potatoes, thinly sliced

Wash watercress, chop, and put in covered pot with 3 tablespoons butter or margarine. Add 3 cups milk and potatoes. Simmer gently until potatoes are cooked. Place in blender on low speed to puree or rub through a sieve. Thin to desired consistency with additional milk. Add 2 tablespoons butter. Pour in soup tureen and garnish with fresh watercress.

Vichyssoise

12 SERVINGS

4 leeks, sliced
1 medium onion, sliced
¼ cup butter
5 medium potatoes, peeled and thinly sliced
4 cups chicken broth
1 tablespoon salt
2 cups milk
2 cups light cream
1 cup whipping cream
Snipped chives, to garnish

Sauté leeks and onion in butter until transparent. Add potatoes, broth, and salt. Simmer for 30 to 40 minutes. Rub through fine sieve and return to heat. Add milk and light cream. Season to taste.

Bring to a boil and then cool. Rub through a fine sieve. Stir in whipping cream.

Chill thoroughly before serving. Garnish with chives.

Cranberry and Orange Soup

Cranberry and Orange Soup

6 SERVINGS

1 pound fresh cranberries
2 cups light chicken stock
1 1/2 cups white wine
2 to 3 pieces lemon rind
Pared rind of ripe orange
1/2 cinnamon stick
1/4 to 1/2 cup sugar, to taste
Juice of 2 oranges
Juice of 1/2 lemon
2 envelopes gelatin (if soup is to be jelled)
6 orange slices, to garnish

Wash cranberries. Put into saucepan with chicken stock and white wine. Add lemon and orange rind and cinnamon stick. Simmer for approximately 10 minutes, until cranberries soften. Put fruit and juice through a fine sieve or a food mill after removing cinnamon stick. Sweeten to taste and add orange and lemon juice.

To serve jelled, soften contents of two envelopes of gelatin according to package directions. Add softened gelatin after soup has been sieved. Re-heat the soup while blending in gelatin.

Serve chilled or jelled with a thin slice of orange as garnish.

Orange Beet Soup

6 SERVINGS

3 cups beets, grated
4 1/2 cups beef bouillon
1 1/2 cups tomato juice
1 teaspoon salt
1/2 teaspoon thyme
1/2 teaspoon pepper
1 cup orange juice, freshly squeezed and strained
Sour cream, to garnish
Chopped chives, to garnish

Simmer beets and bouillon in a 4-quart enamel or stainless steel pot for 20 minutes. Lift out beets with slotted spoon and add remaining ingredients to liquid.

To serve, garnish with sour cream and chopped chives. Can be served hot or cold.

Grapefruit with Crab

Grapefruit with Crab

2 SERVINGS

2 grapefruit
1 cup crab meat, cartilage removed
Mayonnaise, to taste
Parsley or lemon slices, to garnish

Mix flesh from the grapefruit with 1 cup crab meat. Add mayonnaise and seasoning to taste. Serve in the grapefruit shells, garnished with parsley or lemon slices.

Seafood Chowder

8 SERVINGS

2 strips bacon, chopped
1 medium onion, chopped
3 celery ribs, chopped
12 fresh chowder clams with liquid
3/4 pound skinless fresh flounder fillet
2 medium potatoes, quartered and diced
1 to 1 1/4 cups water
1 teaspoon salt
1/4 teaspoon pepper
1/2 teaspoon parsley flakes
1/4 teaspoon sugar
2 cups half-and-half cream
1 teaspoon extra dry sherry
Paprika, to garnish

Sauté bacon until crisp. Add onion and celery to bacon and sauté until tender. Add clams and clam liquid, fish, potatoes, water, and seasonings. Cover and simmer for 20 minutes or more or until fish flakes.

Add half-and-half and heat slowly to near boiling while stirring gently. Remove from heat and add sherry. Sprinkle with paprika to serve. Best when served warm, not hot.

Zucchini Soup

4 SERVINGS

2 tablespoons butter
1/4 cup onion, chopped
1 garlic clove, slivered
3 bouillon cubes
2 cups water
Dash of white pepper
1 teaspoon salt
2 cups zucchini, chopped
1 medium carrot, chopped
2 medium tomatoes, chopped
Sour cream, to garnish
Parsley or chives, to garnish

Sauté onion and garlic in butter until onion is transparent. Stir in remaining ingredients. Heat to boiling, reduce heat and simmer, uncovered, until vegetables are tender, approximately 15 minutes.

Cool slightly, pour mixture into blender and cover. Blend on high speed until smooth. If thinner consistency is desired, stir in additional water or chicken broth. Cool and refrigerate until ice cold. To serve, garnish with sour cream and snipped parsley or chives.

Sweet and Sour Meat Balls

8 DOZEN MEAT BALLS

Meatballs:
1 pound ground beef
1 pound ground veal
2 eggs
2 garlic cloves, crushed
1 hard seedless roll, soaked in water and squeezed dry
Chopped parsley, to taste
Salt and pepper, to taste
1 onion, minced
2 tablespoons butter
Sauce:
6 tablespoons oil
6 tablespoons vinegar
6 tablespoons lemon juice
6 tablespoons sugar
4 cups consommé

Mix together beef, veal, eggs, garlic, roll, parsley, salt, and pepper. Sauté minced onion briefly in butter and add to meat mixture. Shape into small balls. Sauté until browned.

Combine sauce ingredients. Cover meat balls with sauce. Simmer 15 to 20 minutes.

Pickled Garden Appetizer

6 SERVINGS

1/2 small head cauliflower, cut in flowerettes and sliced
2 carrots, pared and cut in 2-inch strips
2 ribs celery, cut in 1-inch pieces
1 green pepper, cut in 2-inch strips
1 4-ounce jar pimentos, drained and cut in strips
1 3-ounce jar pitted green olives, drained
3/4 cup wine vinegar
1/2 cup olive or salad oil
2 tablespoons sugar
1 teaspoon salt
1/2 teaspoon oregano
1/4 teaspoon pepper
1/4 cup water

Combine all ingredients in large skillet. Bring to a boil, stirring occasionally. Reduce heat, cover, and simmer for 5 minutes.

Remove from heat and cool; then refrigerate for at least 24 hours. Drain well before serving.

Mock Borscht

6 SERVINGS

4 cups meat stock
4 cups water
1/4 pound bacon rind, cubed
1 cup carrots, shredded
1/4 cup celery, chopped
1/4 cup green pepper, chopped
2 garlic cloves, slivered
2 medium onions, quartered
1 8-ounce can tomatoes
1/8 teaspoon freshly ground black pepper
1 tablespoon parsley
1 medium raw potato, diced in 1-inch cubes
1/4 medium head cabbage, thinly sliced
1 cup beets, julienned
Salt, to taste

Mix stock and water in heavy pot. Add bacon rind and all vegetables except potatoes cabbage and beets. Bring to fast boil and allow to cook at a rolling boil for 30 minutes.

Add potatoes and boil for another 30 minutes. Stir in thinly sliced cabbage. Boil for 15 minutes. Add beets and salt. Bring to boil again, and boil for 5 minutes. Remove bacon rind. Chill. Serve cold in individual bowls, topped with large spoonful of sour cream.

VEGETABLES & SALADS

Spinach Salad

2 SERVINGS

1/2 pound fresh spinach
Dressing:
1/3 cup olive oil
1/4 cup red wine vinegar
2 tablespoons red wine
1 teaspoon Worcestershire sauce
1 teaspoon prepared mustard
1 teaspoon sugar
Garnish:
4 slices bacon, crisp and crumbled
1 hard-boiled egg, sieved
1/3 red onion, diced

Wash spinach thoroughly and dry.
To make dressing, heat olive oil, vinegar, and wine. Add Worcestershire sauce, mustard, and sugar. Pour over spinach. Sprinkle bacon, egg, and onion over salad. Serve at room temperature.

Molded Beets

4 SERVINGS

1 package lemon gelatin
1 cup boiling water
1/4 cup beet juice
3 tablespoons vinegar
1/2 teaspoon salt
1 teaspoon onion juice
2 tablespoons horseradish
1 cup beets, diced or shredded

Dissolve gelatin in boiling water. Combine remaining ingredients and pour into 4 cup mold. Chil until set.

Romaine Salad with Feta Cheese

6 SERVINGS

1 large head romaine lettuce
Dressing:
1/2 cup olive oil
3 tablespoons red wine vinegar
1/2 teaspoon salt
Freshly ground pepper
1/2 teaspoon oregano
1 garlic clove, peeled
2 ripe avocados, peeled and cut into strips
3/4 cup ripe olives, pitted
1/2 cup feta cheese, crumbled

Wash romaine well and break into small pieces.
To make dressing, whisk together olive oil, vinegar, salt, pepper, oregano, and garlic clove.
Just before serving toss romaine with avocados, olives and feta cheese. Discard garlic before adding dressing.

Shrimp and Avocado Salad

4 SERVINGS

Dressing:
1 tablespoon white vinegar
1 1/2 tablespoons olive oil
1/2 teaspoon Dijon-style mustard
1/2 cup yogurt
1 large garlic clove, peeled and finely chopped
1 tablespoon picante or taco sauce
Dash of hot pepper sauce
Salt and freshly ground pepper, to taste
Juice of 1/2 lemon
Salad:
1 large avocado, peeled and cubed
Juice of 1/2 lemon
1 pound large, fresh shrimp, peeled, deveined and
    cooked
1 small white onion, finely chopped
Lettuce leaves, to garnish

Mix dressing ingredients together in small bowl. Put avocado in large bowl and sprinkle with lemon juice. Add shrimp and onion. Pour enough dressing over shrimp mixture to bind; then gently toss. Serve on top of lettuce leaves.

American Farm Scenes No. 1

The Western Farmer's Home

Spring Salad

4 SERVINGS

½ head cauliflower, broken or sliced
2 carrots, pared and cut in 2-inch pieces
2 ribs celery, cut in 1-inch pieces on bias
1 green pepper, cut in strips
1 4-ounce jar pimentos, drained and chopped
1 3-ounce jar green olives, pitted and drained
¾ cup wine vinegar
½ cup oil
2 tablespoons sugar
1 teaspoon salt
½ teaspoon oregano
¼ teaspoon pepper
½ cup water

Combine all ingredients in a large skillet. Bring to a boil, stirring occasionally. Reduce heat and simmer, covered, for 5 minutes. Cool and refrigerate for 24 hours.

Italian Mixed Vegetables

4 SERVINGS

3 slices bacon, diced
1 medium onion, peeled and sliced
1 red pepper, seeded and cut into strips
3 carrots, peeled and sliced
2 medium potatoes, peeled and diced
½ cup chicken broth
1 10-ounce package frozen tiny peas
Salt and pepper, to taste

In large saucepan, sauté bacon until crisp. Remove with slotted spoon and reserve. Add onion and sauté for 2 minutes. Add pepper, carrots, potatoes, and chicken broth; bring to a boil. Reduce heat to low and cook, covered, for 15 minutes until vegetables are tender but crisp. Add peas and simmer for 5 minutes. Season with salt and pepper and sprinkle with bacon before serving.

Hot Bean Salad

6 SERVINGS

½ pound fresh green beans
½ pound fresh wax beans
½ cup onion, sliced
1 teaspoon salt
1 cup water
2 tablespoons margarine
1 tablespoon cornstarch
1 tablespoon brown sugar
¼ cup cider vinegar
1 15¼-ounce can red kidney beans, drained

Cut fresh beans in 1½-inch pieces. Combine fresh beans, onion, salt and water in saucepan. Bring to a boil. Cover and cook for 8 minutes until beans are tender but crisp. Drain and reserve liquid, adding water if necessary, to make ¾ cup.

In skillet, melt margarine over low heat; stir in cornstarch until smooth. Remove from heat.

Gradually stir ¾ cup reserved liquid into cornstarch mixture until smooth; add brown sugar. Bring to boil over medium heat, stirring constantly, and boil for 1 minute. Stir in vinegar, cooked vegetables, and kidney beans. Simmer 1 to 2 minutes to heat through. Serve immediately.

Dill Pickle Salad

4 SERVINGS

1 cup dill pickle slices
½ cup sweet pickle slices
4 potatoes, cooked, peeled, and cubed
1 9-ounce package frozen green beans, cooked and chilled
1 16-ounce can sliced beets, drained
4 hard-boiled eggs, quartered
Vinaigrette Dressing:
½ cup vegetable oil
¼ cup lemon juice
3 tablespoons sweet pickle liquid
2 tablespoons onion, finely minced
1½ teaspoons sugar
½ teaspoon salt

Combine pickles, potatoes, green beans, beets, and eggs.

Mix dressing ingredients together well.

Toss well with dressing and arrange on large platter to serve.

Greek Salad

4 SERVINGS

1 head broccoli
8 radishes, sliced
8 black olives
Preferred marinade
½ cup pine nuts
½ pound feta cheese
4 cherry tomatoes
Dressing:
½ cup olive oil
3 tablespoons vinegar
½ teaspoon salt
Pepper, to taste
1 garlic clove, minced

Break off small broccoli flowerettes. Peel skin from broccoli stems and slice stems in food processor. Marinate broccoli, radishes, and olives for 5 hours. Add pine nuts, feta cheese and tomatoes. Mix dressing ingredients and toss with salad to serve.

Mixed Vegetables with Artichokes

4 SERVINGS

1 large or 2 medium artichokes
1 lemon
4 small carrots, sliced lengthwise
1 cup small white onions
½ cup mushrooms, cut in half
½ cup celery, sliced
2 tablespoons butter
¼ cup dry white wine
¼ teaspoon thyme
¼ teaspoon marjoram
Salt and pepper, to taste

Bend back outer leaves of artichoke until they snap off easily near base. The edible portion of the leaves should remain on artichoke heart. Continue to snap off and discard thick leaves until central core of pale green leaves is reached. Trim approximately 1 inch off top of artichoke; discard.

Cut artichokes lengthwise into 6 pieces. Trim outer dark green layer from artichoke bottom. Cut out center leaves and choke. Discard. Rub all surfaces with lemon.

Sauté carrots, onions, mushrooms, and celery in butter approximately 5 minutes or until golden. Add wine and seasonings. Stir together over medium heat for 1 minute. Add artichokes and simmer, covered, for 25 minutes or until tender.

Asparagus Salad

6 SERVINGS

20 asparagus spears, chopped
2 large heads Bibb lettuce
2 tablespoons parsley, minced
1 tablespoon shallots, minced
Mustard French Dressing:
2 tablespoons Dijon-style mustard
Salt and pepper, to taste
3 tablespoons red wine vinegar
1/2 cup olive oil
1 egg yolk, hard-boiled and sieved, to garnish
Minced parsley, to garnish

Cook asparagus in rapidly boiling, salted water for 5 to 10 minutes, or until just tender. Drain immediately and dry well.
Tear lettuce into pieces, reserving some whole leaves to line salad bowl. Mix torn lettuce with parsley and shallots.
Combine dressing ingredients. Toss 1/2 cup of dressing with lettuce, parsley, and shallots. Toss asparagus with remaining dressing. Line a shallow bowl with reserved lettuce leaves. Combine asparagus pieces and lettuce, and arrange in salad bowl. Sprinkle salad with hard-boiled egg yolk and minced parsley.

Tomatoes and Cucumbers with Green Dressing

4 SERVINGS

Lettuce leaves, to garnish
4 large tomatoes, sliced
2 medium cucumbers, peeled and sliced
Salt and pepper, to taste
2 teaspoons lemon juice
Dressing:
1 ripe avocado
1/2 cup sour cream
1/2 cup plain yogurt
2 tablespoons parsley, minced
2 tablespoons chives, chopped

Arrange lettuce leaves on platter, with tomatoes and cucumbers on top. Salt and pepper lightly and sprinkle with 1 teaspoon lemon juice. Chill until serving.
To make dressing, scoop out avocado flesh and mash well with 1 teaspoon lemon juice. Mix with sour cream and yogurt until smooth. Stir in parsley and chives. Serve with tomatoes and cucumbers.

Sour Cream Cucumber Salad

4 SERVINGS

2 to 3 large cucumbers, thinly sliced
1 onion, thinly sliced and separated into rings
1 tablespoon salt
1/4 teaspoon pepper
1/2 cup vinegar
1 cup sour cream
Tomatoes, quartered, to garnish

Combine all ingredients except sour cream in large bowl. Place smaller bowl on top as weight. Refrigerate for several hours. Drain well. Add sour cream and mix thoroughly. Serve with quartered tomatoes.

Mediterranean Rice Salad

8 SERVINGS

1/2 cup vinaigrette dressing
4 cups cooked rice
1/4 cup green onion, chopped
1/2 cup radishes, thinly sliced
1/2 cup pine nuts, lightly toasted
1/2 cup black olives, pitted and sliced
Red leaf lettuce, to line serving bowl
Chopped parsley, to garnish

Toss dressing with rice while rice is still hot. Chill. Mix remaining ingredients with dressed rice. When ready to serve, arrange in bowl lined with red leaf lettuce leaves. Sprinkle with chopped parsley.

Mozzarella and Cherry Tomato Salad

2 SERVINGS

12 cherry tomatoes
12 1-inch cubes mozzarella cheese
1/4 cup olive oil
2 tablespoons wine vinegar
1 teaspoon fresh oregano, chopped
Salt and pepper, to taste

Cut cherry tomatoes in half. Mix in bowl with mozzarella cheese. Drizzle olive oil over tomatoes and cheese to coat. Add vinegar and toss.
Sprinkle oregano over salad. Add salt and pepper to taste and toss again.

The New Brood

Cucumber and Crab

8 SERVINGS

2 small cucumbers
1 tablespoon sesame seeds, to garnish
8 ounces crab meat, cartilage removed
1 cup rice vinegar
½ teaspoon salt
1 tablespoon light soy sauce (or mix 2 teaspoons dark
　　soy sauce with 1 teaspoon water)
1 tablespoon sugar, or to taste
2 thin strips ginger root, peeled and finely sliced, to
　　garnish

Wash and slice unpeeled cucumbers into paper-thin rounds. Salt lightly and place in colander. Put plate on top to press out excess liquid; let stand for 30 minutes.

Toast sesame seeds over low heat until brown and hopping in pan; set aside for garnish.

Rinse cucumbers and squeeze lightly to rid of excess moisture; place in salad bowl to one side. Place crab meat on opposite side of bowl. Mix vinegar, salt, soy sauce, and sugar until salt and sugar have completely dissolved; pour over crab and cucumbers and marinate until serving time. Keep chilled.

Before serving, drain excess dressing. Serve in small dish by arranging small heaps of cucumber and crab meat side by side. Garnish with finely sliced strips of ginger root and toasted sesame seeds.

Cheddar Squash Casserole

8 SERVINGS

5 cups yellow squash, thinly sliced
Salt, to taste
2 egg yolks, slightly beaten
1 cup sour cream
2 tablespoons flour
2 egg whites, stiffly beaten
1½ cups sharp cheddar cheese, shredded
1 tablespoon butter or margarine
¼ cup fine bread crumbs

Pre-heat oven to 350°F.

Simmer squash until tender; drain well. Sprinkle with salt. Combine egg yolks, sour cream, and flour. Fold in egg whites. Place half the squash in a baking dish; top with half the egg mixture and half the cheese. Repeat layers. Melt butter and stir in crumbs; sprinkle over casserole. Bake for 20 to 25 minutes.

Wilted Lettuce

6-8 SERVINGS

4 heads lettuce
12 slices bacon
⅔ cup cider vinegar
½ cup coffee
Salt and pepper, to taste

Wash lettuce thoroughly and break into small pieces. Fry the bacon until crisp, drain and crumble into bits. Drain the bacon fat from the skillet, returning 1 tablespoon to skillet. Add vinegar, coffee, salt and pepper to skillet. Bring to a boil, stirring to combine.

Add lettuce and stir quickly to coat the leaves. Remove from heat and serve immediately.

Creamed Celery

4 SERVINGS

2 stalks celery, approximately 1½ pounds
½ cup cold, salted water
2 tablespoons butter or margarine
1 tablespoon cornstarch
½ teaspoon salt
¼ teaspoon cayenne
2 tablespoons lemon juice
1 cup white wine

Wash celery stalks. Clean off dark spots. Slice into 1-inch pieces and soak in saucepan in salted, cold water for 10 minutes. Cover and cook over medium heat until celery is tender. Drain and set aside.

While celery is cooking, melt butter over low heat, blend in cornstarch, salt, and cayenne; gradually add lemon juice and stir in white wine. Stir constantly until smooth. Bring to a boil and simmer for 2 minutes.

Fold celery pieces into sauce and stir gently until each piece is coated. Simmer for 2 minutes.

Southern Rice

6 SERVINGS

4 to 6 slices bacon, diced
3 cups cooked rice
1 4-ounce can sliced mushrooms, drained
1 cup cooked green peas
1/4 cup pimentos, diced
1 tablespoon chives, chopped
1 teaspoon salt
1/4 teaspoon freshly ground black pepper

In 10-inch skillet sauté bacon until crisp. Drain off fat. Add remaining ingredients to skillet and heat thoroughly.

Broccoli Puree

8 SERVINGS

3 pounds broccoli
6 tablespoons butter
4 tablespoons shallots, minced
4 tablespoons heavy cream
Pinch of nutmeg
Salt and pepper, to taste

Cut flowerettes from broccoli and set aside. Trim tough ends off stalks, peel, and cut into 1-inch pieces. Bring large pot of salted water to boil, add pieces of broccoli stalks and cook for 8 minutes. Add broccoli flowerettes and cook for 4 minutes more. Broccoli should be soft but not mushy. Drain broccoli well and squeeze out as much moisture as possible. Blot with paper towels.

Heat 3 tablespoons butter in small frying pan, add shallots, and sauté over low heat until shallots are soft and transparent. Do not brown. Place shallots and remaining butter into food processor bowl. Add broccoli in batches and process until reduced to puree. Turn puree into saucepan, heat thoroughly, and whisk in cream. Season to taste with nutmeg, salt, and pepper.

Cauliflower with Pimento

4 SERVINGS

2 tablespoons butter
2 tablespoons flour
1/2 teaspoon salt
Pepper, to taste
1 cup hot milk
4 tablespoons pimentos, pureed
1 head cauliflower, cooked

Melt butter in saucepan. Blend flour, salt, and pepper with melted butter. Gradually pour in milk, stirring constantly until thickened. Add pimento puree. Pour over cauliflower before serving.

Marinated Asparagus

4 SERVINGS

2 pounds asparagus spears, cooked
Marinade:
1/2 teaspoon sugar
2/3 cup vegetable oil
4 tablespoons wine vinegar
1/2 teaspoon dry mustard
1/2 teaspoon paprika
Lettuce leaves, for garnish
Pimento strips, for garnish

Combine marinade ingredients and mix well. Marinate asparagus overnight. Drain. Serve on lettuce leaves and garnish with pimento strips.

Boiled Red Potatoes with Mint

6 SERVINGS

12 small red potatoes
Salt for water
2 tablespoons butter, melted
Pepper, to taste
2 tablespoons fresh mint, chopped

Wash potatoes and place them whole in pot of cold water to cover. Bring water to boil, add salt to taste, and cook for 18 minutes or until potatoes are tender. Drain in colander. Cut potatoes in half. Place halves on large platter, drizzle melted butter over them, and sprinkle with pepper and fresh chopped mint.

FISH & SEAFOOD

Shrimp Creole

6 SERVINGS

1 medium green pepper
2 medium onions
1/4 cup peanut oil
1/2 cup celery, diced
1 16-ounce can tomatoes
1/4 cup chili sauce
1/4 cup seedless raisins
1/2 cup slivered almonds
1 bay leaf
1 teaspoon parsley flakes
1/4 teaspoon thyme
1/4 teaspoon curry powder
1/4 teaspoon cayenne pepper
1/4 teaspoon salt
1/4 teaspoon pepper
1 pound cooked shrimp, peeled and deveined

Slice green pepper and onions into thin strips. Heat oil and sauté green pepper, onions, and celery. Add all other ingredients except shrimp and simmer for 50 minutes. Add shrimp and simmer 10 minutes longer. Serve over hot rice.

Fish Fillets with Tomato Sauce and Cheese

2 SERVINGS

2 flounder fillets
Dash of salt and pepper
2 tablespoons onion, chopped
2 slices American cheese
1 6-ounce can tomato sauce

Pre-heat oven to 375°F.
Wipe fillets with dampened paper towel. Sprinkle with salt, pepper, and onion. Place cheese slice at end of each fillet. Roll up and place in greased pan. Pour tomato sauce over fish. Bake for 30 minutes.

Sweet and Sour Fish

4 SERVINGS

3 to 3 1/2 pounds fish fillets
4 tablespoons onions, finely chopped
2 teaspoons ginger root, chopped
Pinch of salt
1/4 teaspoon freshly ground black pepper
1 teaspoon soy sauce
1 teaspoon sherry
1/2 cup cornstarch
Fat, to deep fry
Sweet and Sour Sauce:
3/4 cup cider vinegar
1 tablespoon cornstarch
1 green pepper, julienned
1 carrot, peeled and julienned
2 teaspoons ginger root, chopped
4 scallions, sliced into 1/2-inch pieces
2 tablespoons sweet pickle relish
Salt to taste
1/4 cup sugar

Sprinkle fish with onions, ginger root, salt, pepper, soy sauce, and sherry. Let stand for 30 minutes. Roll in cornstarch; let stand another 10 minutes.
Heat fat in deep fryer or deep skillet over medium-high heat. Fry fish 10 to 15 minutes or until done. Drain fish. Keep warm while preparing sauce.
To make sauce, mix together all ingredients. Cook over low heat, stirring constantly, until thickened. Serve fish with sauce.

Seafood Scampi

8 SERVINGS

3/4 cup butter
8 garlic cloves, crushed
1 pound shrimp, peeled and deveined
1 pound raw fish, cut in chunks
1 pound langostino (1 pound of more shrimp and fish
    can be used if langostino is not available)
1 teaspoon salt
4 spring onions, chopped
1/2 cup parsley, chopped

Heat butter and garlic in frying pan or wok until butter is melted. Add seafood and salt. Cook for 5 minutes, turning seafood constantly. When fish flakes and shrimp are pink, add spring onions and parsley and cook for 2 more minutes. Serve over rice or Chinese noodles.

Caught on the Fly

Baked Fish

3 SERVINGS

1 pound fish fillets
1 tablespoon parsley, chopped
1 tablespoon lemon juice
³⁄₄ teaspoon seasoned salt
3 tablespoons olive oil
1 medium onion, thinly sliced
1 garlic clove, minced
1 large tomato, thinly sliced
3 slices lemon
2 tablespoons white wine

Pre-heat oven to 350°F.
Arrange fish in an 8 or 9-inch square baking dish. Sprinkle with parsley, lemon juice, and seasoned salt. Heat oil in small skillet and sauté onion and garlic until limp. Top fish with onion mixture, including oil from skillet. Arrange tomatoes on top of onion mixture, then place lemon slices between tomatoes. Pour wine over fish and bake for 30 to 35 minutes or until fish flakes with a fork.

Cod with Potatoes and Onions

6 SERVINGS

¹⁄₄ cup olive oil
¹⁄₂ teaspoon finely chopped garlic
4 medium onions, sliced
2 large green peppers, seeded and sliced
Dash of saffron
1 teaspoon paprika
6 medium potatoes, peeled and cut lengthwise ¹⁄₄ inch thick
1¹⁄₂ pounds cod
2 cups boiling water
2 tablespoons parsley, finely chopped
Salt and pepper, to taste

In large skillet, heat oil over moderate heat. Sauté garlic, onion, and green pepper until soft. Add saffron, paprika, potatoes, and cod.
Pour in boiling water to cover contents and simmer, covered, for 30 to 35 minutes. Add parsley, salt and pepper to taste.

Enoch Arden—The Lonely Isle

Grilled Fish Fillets

8 SERVINGS

2 pounds fresh fish fillets
¼ cup French dressing
1 tablespoon lemon juice
1 tablespoon onion, grated
Salt and pepper, to taste

Spread heavy-duty foil on barbecue. Grease lightly to prevent sticking. Mix together French dressing, lemon juice, onion, salt, and pepper and brush on fish. Grill for 20 minutes without turning.

Crab Cakes

6 SERVINGS

1 pound crab meat, cartilage removed
½ cup bread crumbs
Salt and pepper, to taste
1 egg, beaten
1 tablespoon parsley
1 teaspoon dry mustard
2 tablespoons mayonnaise

Gently mix together all ingredients. Shape into cakes and deep fry or broil until brown.

Fried Fish with Mexican Sauce

4 SERVINGS

1 pound firm fish fillets
2 tablespoons lemon juice
1/2 teaspoon salt
1/4 teaspoon pepper
1/2 cup flour
1/4 cup cooking oil
Mexican Sauce:
2 tablespoons olive oil
1 small onion, chopped
1/2 cup green pepper, chopped
1/4 cup celery, chopped
1 garlic clove, minced
1 cup canned tomatoes, drained and chopped
2 tablespoons dry sherry
Salt and pepper, to taste
1 large pinch saffron
2 tablespoons parsley, chopped, to garnish

Sprinkle fish fillets with lemon juice, salt, and pepper; set aside while making sauce.

For Mexican sauce, heat olive oil in saucepan or small skillet. Add onion, green pepper, celery, and garlic; sauté until onion is transparent. Add tomatoes, sherry, salt, and pepper to taste, and saffron, mixing well. Allow sauce to simmer while frying fish.

Drain fish well. Heat cooking oil over moderate heat in large frying pan. Dip fish in flour, coating well; fry until golden, turning once. Drain fish and serve hot, topped with sauce. Garnish with chopped parsley.

Sweet and Pungent Shrimp

4 SERVINGS

1/4 cup brown sugar
2 tablespoons cornstarch
1/2 teaspoon salt
1/4 cup vinegar
1 tablespoon soy sauce
1/4 teaspoon ginger
2 1/2 cups canned pineapple chunks, including syrup
1 green pepper, sliced
2 small onions, sliced
1 pound shrimp, peeled, deveined and cooked

In saucepan, mix sugar, cornstarch, and salt. Add vinegar, soy sauce, ginger, and syrup from pineapple. Simmer until thickened, stirring constantly. Add vegetables and pineapple. Simmer for 2 minutes.

Add shrimp. Bring to boil, stirring constantly. Serve over rice.

Steamed Whole Fish

3 SERVINGS

1 1/2 pounds whole fish
1 teaspoon salt
1/2 teaspoon freshly ground pepper
1/4 teaspoon powdered ginger
3 cups water
2 teaspoons mixed pickling spices
2 bay leaves
2 garlic cloves, cut in half
2 tablespoons scallion, chopped
Garnish:
3 lemon slices
1 tomato, sliced
Parsley, to taste

Lightly score fish skin. Combine salt, pepper, and ginger and rub on fish thoroughly.

Pour water into large frying pan or wok and add pickling spices, bay leaves, garlic, and scallion. Place rack in pan or wok so that fish will sit above liquid, allowing steam to circulate. Place fish on rack, cover, and simmer for approximately 30 minutes, or until tender. Garnish with lemon slices, tomato, and parsley.

Fish Fillets Stuffed with Mushrooms

4 SERVINGS

1 pound fresh mushrooms
2 tablespoons onion, chopped
1 small garlic clove, minced
2 tablespoons butter or margarine
3 tablespoons parsley, chopped
1 1/2 pounds fillet of sole or flounder
Salt and pepper, to taste
1 10 1/2 ounce can of shrimp soup, undiluted
Grated Parmesan cheese, to garnish

Clean mushrooms. Sauté onions, mushrooms, and garlic in butter for 3 to 5 minutes. Add 2 tablespoons of chopped parsley.

Season fillets with salt and pepper. Place sautéed mixture on fillets and roll up. Fasten with toothpicks.

Place fillets in large skillet. Pour shrimp soup over. Cover and simmer 7 to 10 minutes. Do not allow to boil.

To serve, garnish with remaining parsley and grated cheese.

Cioppino

12 SERVINGS

1 large onion, chopped
5 cloves garlic, minced
3 tablespoons olive oil
3 1-pound cans tomatoes
1 1/2 cups tomato sauce
2 large bay leaves
2 tablespoons parsley, minced
1 teaspoon salt
1 teaspoon basil
1/4 teaspoon pepper
2 cups red wine
20 mussels, in shell
40 clams, in shell
4 pounds large shrimp, peeled and deveined
5 lobsters, cut in half, or 10 lobster tails
2 pounds scallops

Using large Dutch oven with a high lid, sauté onion and garlic in olive oil until transparent. Stir in tomatoes, tomato sauce, bay leaves, parsley, salt, basil, and pepper. Bring to a boil, reduce heat and simmer, covered, for 2 hours.

While sauce simmers, scrub mussels thoroughly with stiff brush. Wash clams under running water and rinse several times to remove sand.

Stir wine into sauce. Add shrimp and lobsters. Simmer, covered, for 10 minutes. Place scallops carefully in sauce. Layer clams and mussels on top of mixture. Cover and steam for 10 minutes or until shells are fully opened. Ladle into large, deep soup bowls and serve with French bread.

Fish Loaf

4 SERVINGS

2 slices white bread
1 cup milk
2 eggs
1 pound fillet of haddock
3/4 teaspoon salt
1/4 teaspoon pepper
1/2 teaspoon sugar
1 large onion, chopped
1 rib celery, chopped
1 carrot, chopped
Sprig of parsley, to garnish

Pre-heat oven to 375°F.
Soak bread in milk. Add eggs, haddock, seasonings, and remaining ingredients. Place in greased loaf pan. Bake for 1 hour. Garnish with parsley.

Sesame Salmon

3 SERVINGS

3 salmon steaks, cut into thirds
1 green pepper, cut into thin strips
1 leek, cut into thin strips
2 garlic cloves, minced
1/2 red chili pepper, minced
1 tablespoon sesame seeds
2 teaspoons vinegar
1 tablespoon sesame seed oil
2 tablespoons soy sauce
2 teaspoons sugar
3 tablespoons water

Pre-heat oven to 400°F.
Combine all ingredients except salmon. Marinate salmon in mixture for 45 minutes. Lift each salmon out of marinade with slotted spoon. Wrap each piece of fish in foil and bake until tender, approximately 20 to 25 minutes.

Crab Imperial

4 SERVINGS

3 tablespoons margarine or butter
1 tablespoon flour
1/2 cup milk
1 teaspoon onion, minced
1 1/2 teaspoons Worcestershire sauce
2 slices white bread, cubed, and crusts removed
1/2 cup mayonnaise
1 tablespoon lemon juice
1/2 teaspoon salt
Dash of pepper
1 pound crabmeat, cartilage removed
Paprika, to garnish

Pre-heat oven to 450°F.
In medium saucepan, melt 1 tablespoon margarine or butter; stir in flour. Slowly add milk, stirring constantly. Stir over medium heat until mixture comes to a boil and thickens. Mix in onion, Worcestershire sauce, and bread cubes. Remove from heat to cool. Fold in mayonnaise, lemon juice, salt, and pepper.
In another saucepan, melt remaining 2 tablespoons margarine or butter until lightly browned. Add crabmeat and toss lightly. Combine with sauce mixture. Place in individual shells or greased 1-quart casserole. Bake for 10 to 15 minutes, or until bubbly and lightly browned on top.

Lamb Kebabs with Orange

MEATS

Lamb Kebabs with Orange

6 SERVINGS

2 pounds lamb, boned
2 small onions, peeled and quartered
Fresh rosemary, to taste
Marinade:
1 cup brown sugar
1 16-ounce can frozen orange juice concentrate
4 tablespoons Worcestershire sauce
1 teaspoon prepared mustard
Juice of 1 lemon
1 tablespoon cornstarch

Trim excess fat from meat and cut into pieces. Place onion quarters on skewers alternately with pieces of meat, and occasional leaves of fresh rosemary.
Put sugar, orange juice, and Worcestershire sauce into saucepan. Mix mustard with lemon juice. Add to saucepan and stir over low heat until sugar dissolves. Brush kebabs liberally with marinade. Place over hot coals on barbecue rack, and cook for approximately 10 to 15 minutes, turning and basting frequently.
Blend cornstarch with a little water, add to remaining marinade, and stir until boiling. Season to taste and serve as a sauce with the kebabs.

Teriyaki

Teriyaki

8 SERVINGS

2½ to 3 pounds sirloin steak, cut about ½ inch thick
(Pork or chicken may be substituted for steak)
1 cup soy sauce
⅓ cup dry sherry
4 tablespoons brown sugar
1½ teaspoons ground ginger
2 teaspoons grated onion
1 garlic clove, crushed
18 chunks canned pineapple
18 small mushroom caps
2 tablespoons pineapple juice
1 tablespoon cornstarch

Cut steak into 1-inch squares.

Mix together soy sauce, sherry, sugar, ginger, onion, and garlic. Add meat and marinate for 3 hours.

Place steak, pineapple, and mushrooms on skewers, starting and finishing with a piece of meat. Cook for about 4 to 5 minutes over hot coals, turning once or twice to brown evenly.

Mix pineapple juice slowly into cornstarch, add marinade and simmer, stirring constantly until sauce thickens. Serve with kebabs.

Veal Marsala

8 SERVINGS

16 pieces veal scallopini, pounded thin
1/2 cup flour
6 tablespoons butter
4 tablespoons oil
1 1/2 pounds mushrooms, thickly sliced
Salt and pepper, to taste
1 1/2 cups chicken broth
3/4 cup marsala wine

Pre-heat oven to 150°F. Coat one side only of each veal scallopini with flour. Melt 4 tablespoons butter with oil in large skillet over high heat. Sauté veal, uncoated side first, in batches. Cook on each side only until veal is slightly browned. Add additional butter and oil to pan if necessary.

Remove veal to large serving platter and place in 150°F oven. Add remaining 2 tablespoons butter to skillet and sauté mushroom slices for 5 minutes. Add salt and pepper to taste.

Arrange mushrooms over veal on platter and return to oven. Deglaze skillet with broth and wine over high heat, scraping up browned bits. Bring to boil and pour over veal. Finished veal may be held in low oven for up to 1 hour.

This recipe can also be made with turkey cutlets. If using turkey, do not flour before cooking.

Creole Ham

4 SERVINGS

1 onion, chopped
3 tablespoons butter
1 green pepper, chopped
1 8-ounce can tomatoes
1 cup washed rice
2 cups water
Salt, to taste
Pepper, to taste
Paprika, to taste
2 cups ham, cooked and diced

Brown onion in butter, add pepper and tomatoes. Bring to a boil. Add rice and water and simmer until rice is tender. Stir in salt, pepper and paprika to taste. Add ham, and simmer until thoroughly heated.

Beef Burgundy

5 SERVINGS

1 1/2 pounds beef tenderloin strips
3 tablespoons margarine
1 medium onion, chopped
1 green pepper, chopped
1 8-ounce can consommé
2 tablespoons cornstarch
1 cup burgundy wine
Salt and pepper, to taste

Brown meat in margarine. Remove from pan. Sauté vegetables until soft. Add consommé. Stir cornstarch into wine, add to consommé, and heat slowly, stirring until mixture bubbles. Season to taste with salt and pepper.

Add beef strips and heat thoroughly.

Meat Balls

6 SERVINGS

1 pound veal, finely ground
1/2 pound pork, finely ground
1 small onion, grated
4 tablespoons flour
1 teaspoon salt
1/8 teaspoon pepper
1 egg, beaten
1 1/4 cups milk
Butter, to brown

Mix together veal, pork, onion, flour, salt, and pepper. Add egg and milk a little at a time. Mix thoroughly until all ingredients are absorbed into meat.

Melt a little butter in skillet. Form meat balls and drop meat balls into hot fat. Cook for approximately 10 minutes until brown on all sides.

POULTRY

Hawaiian Chicken

6 SERVINGS

2 cups barbecue sauce
1/4 cup wine vinegar
1 teaspoon rosemary
1 teaspoon oregano
1 large clove garlic, minced
Salt and pepper, to taste
1/2 cup brown sugar
Juice of 1 lemon
3 pounds chicken, cut up
2 cups pineapple chunks
1 cup mandarin oranges
1 cup slivered almonds

Mix barbecue sauce, vinegar, rosemary, oregano, garlic, salt, pepper, brown sugar, and lemon juice. Add chicken and marinate overnight.

Bake, covered, for 1 hour at 300°F. During final 15 minutes of baking, add pineapple, oranges, and almonds.

Chicken with Tomatoes and Chick Peas

6 SERVINGS

2 pounds boned chicken breasts and thighs
1/4 cup olive oil
1/2 pound mushrooms, sliced
1 16-ounce can chick peas
2 tomatoes, chopped
2 green peppers, chopped
5 garlic cloves, minced
2 teaspoons paprika
1 1/2 cups white wine
2 pinches of salt
2 pinches of black pepper

Boil chicken for 15 minutes. Drain, cool, and cut in bite-size pieces.

In a large, heavy skillet, combine olive oil, chicken, mushrooms, chick peas, tomatoes, green pepper, garlic, and paprika. Simmer for 30 minutes.

Add white wine, salt, and black pepper and simmer for five minutes before serving.

Hungarian Roast Duck

6 SERVINGS

4 to 5 pounds whole dressed duck
Garlic salt and pepper, to taste
2 tablespoons paprika
2 apples, quartered
2 onions, quartered
10 slices bacon, 8 raw; 2 cooked and crumbled
1/4 cup butter, melted
3 cups sauerkraut
4 juniper berries
2 teaspoons caraway seeds

Pre-heat oven to 350°F.

Sprinkle ducks inside and out with garlic salt, pepper, and paprika. Place apple and onion quarters in cavities of bird, then place in baking pan breast up. Lay strips of raw bacon on breasts to prevent ducks from drying out. Roast for approximately 1 hour and 15 minutes, basting frequently with butter.

Combine sauerkraut, juniper berries, caraway seeds, and crumbled bacon in shallow casserole and heat in oven 20 minutes before duck is done.

Carve duck and place on sauerkraut mixture.

Brunswick Stew

10 SERVINGS

1 stewing hen, 6 pounds, or 2 broiler-fryers, 3 pounds each
2 to 3 quarts water
2 large onions, sliced
2 cups okra, cut
4 cups fresh tomatoes
2 cups lima beans
3 medium potatoes, diced
4 cups corn
3 teaspoons salt
1 teaspoon pepper
1 tablespoon sugar

Cut chicken into pieces and simmer in 3 quarts of water for thin stew, or 2 quarts for thick stew, until meat can be easily removed from bones, approximately 2 hours and 15 minutes. Remove chicken and set aside.

Add raw vegetables to broth and simmer uncovered, until beans and potatoes are tender. Stir occasionally to prevent scorching. Add chicken, boned and diced if desired, and seasonings. Flavor improves if refrigerated overnight and reheated the next day.

Chicken Sorrento

6 SERVINGS

1 chicken, 3 to 3 1/2 pounds
Flour, for dredging
3 tablespoons oil
1/3 cup rice
1 large onion, peeled
1 orange, unpeeled, halved and seeded
1/2 cup milk
1 cup water
3 tablespoons chopped pimento
1/4 teaspoon thyme
Pinch of sugar
Pinch of cayenne pepper

Pre-heat oven to 350°F.

Cut chicken into pieces and season to taste. Dredge in flour.

Heat oil in skillet, and brown chicken on all sides. Remove from pan and set aside. Put rice into skillet and stir over low heat until rice is brown.

Put onion and unpeeled orange through a food grinder, using the coarse blade. Combine with rice. Put onion, orange and rice mixture into casserole. Arrange chicken on top. Add milk, water and the remainder of the ingredients.

Cover and bake for 1 hour to 1 hour and 15 minutes.

Garden, Orchard and Vine

The Cream of Love

DESSERTS

Peanut Butter Nuggets

3 DOZEN COOKIES

1 cup peanut butter
1 teaspoon lemon juice
1/4 teaspoon salt
1 1/2 cups condensed milk
1 cup chopped seedless raisins

Pre-heat oven to 375°F.
Mix together peanut butter, lemon juice, and salt. Gradually stir in condensed milk. Add raisins. Drop in teaspoons onto greased baking sheets; bake for 10 minutes.

Easy Chocolate Bars

24 BARS

2 cups raisins
3/4 cup crunchy peanut butter
5 tablespoons cocoa
1 tablespoon butter
1 teaspoon vanilla
3 cups quick-cooking oatmeal
Syrup:
2 cups brown sugar, packed
1/2 cup evaporated milk
1/4 cup margarine

Stir together raisins, peanut butter, cocoa and butter in a large bowl. Stir in oatmeal and set aside.
Boil syrup ingredients together in a large saucepan for 1 minute.
Stir syrup into raisin mixture. Grease an 8-inch square pan with butter. Press mixture into pan and chill at least 1 hour.

Orange Cake

2 8-INCH SQUARE CAKE LAYERS

¾ cup shortening
1½ cups sugar
2 teaspoons orange rind
3 eggs
2½ cups cake flour
2¼ teaspoons baking powder
⅜ teaspoon salt
¾ cup orange juice
Frosting:
1 egg white
1 cup sugar
¼ teaspoon cream of tartar
5 marshmallows, chopped
⅓ cup boiling water
Dash of lemon juice
1 cup coconut

Pre-heat oven to 350°F.
Cream together shortening, sugar, and orange rind. Add eggs, one at a time, beating after each. Sift flour, baking powder and salt together. Add flour mixture alternately with orange juice.
Pour into 2 8-inch square greased and floured pans for 25 to 30 minutes. Cool for 5 minutes, remove from pans and cool completely on cake rack.
To make frosting, beat together egg white, sugar, cream of tartar, marshmallows, and water at high speed for 5 minutes. Add lemon juice.
Frost cooled cake layers. Cover with coconut that has been toasted in oven at 325°F. until golden brown.

Yogurt Cheese Pie

8 SERVINGS

Crust:
1¼ cups graham cracker crumbs
¼ cup sugar
¼ cup softened butter or margarine
1 teaspoon ground cinnamon
Filling:
12 ounces ricotta or farmer cheese
1½ cups plain yogurt
3 tablespoons honey
1 teaspoon vanilla extract

Pre-heat oven to 375°F.
Combine crust ingredients and press evenly into 9-inch pie pan. Bake for 5 minutes; cool.
Beat cheese well. Add yogurt gradually, mixing well. Stir in honey and vanilla. Pour into pie shell and refrigerate at least 24 hours before serving.

Meringues

6 MERINGUES

3 egg whites
Pinch of salt
1 cup sugar
¼ teaspoon vinegar
Vanilla and almond extracts, to taste

Pre-heat oven to 275°F.
Beat egg whites and salt until whites stand in stiff peaks. Gradually add sugar, 1 tablespoon at a time, beating well after each addition. Add vinegar and extracts.
Shape into small rounds on greased cookie sheet, scooping out a hollow into each (shells should be 2½ to 3 inches in diameter). Place 2 inches apart. Bake until light brown.
Meringues can be filled with fresh fruits, ice cream or sherbert and topped as desired.

Almond Cookies

4 DOZEN COOKIES

½ cup butter
½ cup white sugar
½ tablespoon molasses
1 cup all-purpose flour
2 cups rolled oats
½ cup flaked almonds
1 teaspoon baking soda
¼ cup boiling water

Pre-heat oven to 375°F.
Cream butter and sugar. Add molasses and mix well. Stir in flour, rolled oats, and almonds.
Dissolve baking soda in boiling water and add to mixture while hot. Mix to stiff dough. Roll teaspoons of dough into balls; place on greased baking pans, allowing room to spread. Press flat; decorate top of each cookie with flaked almond. Bake for 15 minutes. Remove to cooling tray. Store when cold.

Lemon Pudding

4 SERVINGS

3 eggs, separated
Rind of ½ orange, grated
Juice of ½ lemon
1 cup sugar
2 tablespoons cake flour
1 cup milk
Pinch of salt

Pre-heat oven to 350°F.
Beat egg yolks. Stir in orange rind and lemon juice. Combine sugar and flour and add to mixture. Add milk slowly. Beat egg whites with a pinch of salt until stiff, and fold into batter. Pour into greased casserole and place in pan of cold water. Bake for 45 minutes.

Fried Crullers

24 CRULLERS

2 eggs, beaten
1 cup sugar
1/4 cup butter, melted
1 cup sour milk
4 cups all-purpose flour
1/4 teaspoon baking soda
4 teaspoons baking powder
1/2 teaspoon salt
1/2 teaspoon nutmeg
1 teaspoon cinnamon

Mix together eggs, sugar, butter and milk. Combine dry ingredients and sift into liquid ingredients, mixing well. Turn onto floured surface and form into long roll. Cut in slices and deep-fry each side in 375°F. oil. Drain on paper towels.

Apple Cobbler

6 SERVINGS

4 cups baking apples, peeled and sliced
1 1/3 cups sugar
1/8 teaspoon cinnamon
1/2 teaspoon almond extract
2 tablespoons butter
Topping:
1 1/2 cups sifted flour
2 teaspoons baking powder
1/2 teaspoon salt
1/4 cup butter
1 egg, beaten
2/3 cup milk

Pre-heat oven to 425°F.
Place apples in 1½-quart baking dish. Sprinkle with 1 cup sugar, cinnamon, and almond extract and dot with butter. Sift together flour, baking powder, ⅓ cup sugar, and salt. Cut in butter until mixture is slightly coarser than cornmeal.
Combine egg and milk; pour into dry ingredients. Stir just enough to mix. Spoon over apples in baking dish. Bake for 30 minutes, until browned.
Serve with fresh cream, sour cream, or ice cream.

Cheese Cookies

8 DOZEN COOKIES

2 cups cheddar cheese, grated
1 cup soft butter
2 cups flour, sifted
1 teaspoon salt

Cream cheese and butter together. Add flour and salt and mix until dough is smooth and well-blended. Shape dough into rolls, about 1 inch in diameter. Chill for 2 hours, or until dough is firm.
Pre-heat oven to 350°F.
Slice dough into thin rounds and place on ungreased baking sheets at least 1 inch apart. Bake for 12 to 15 minutes.

Raisin Cake

1 9 × 13-INCH CAKE

2 cups water
2/3 cup vegetable oil
1/2 cup raisins
2 cups sugar
1 teaspoon cinnamon
1/4 teaspoon nutmeg
1/2 teaspoon cloves
1/2 teaspoon allspice
2 teaspoons baking soda
2 eggs, beaten separately
3 cups sifted flour

Preheat at oven to 350°F.
Combine water, vegetable oil, raisins, sugar and spices in saucepan. Boil for 3 minutes, then cool. When cool, put in large bowl and add baking soda, beaten eggs, one at a time, and flour. Mix well. Pour into 9 × 13-inch pan and bake for 30 minutes.

Spiced Pears

6 SERVINGS

6 Anjou pears
4 cups sugar
2 cups water
1 stick cinnamon
3 to 4 whole cloves
1 cup sour cream

Peel and core pears. Combine sugar, water, cinnamon stick, and cloves in deep saucepan. Simmer over low heat until sugar is dissolved. Place pears in syrup and simmer for 15 minutes or until tender.
Serve with sour cream.

American Country Life—Summer's Evening

Summer

SOUPS & APPETIZERS

Gazpacho

6 SERVINGS

1/2 cup olive oil
4 teaspoons lemon juice
6 cups tomato juice
3 cups tomatoes, diced
2 cups beef broth
1/2 cup onions, finely minced
2 cups celery, finely minced
1 teaspoon Tabasco sauce
2 tablespoons salt
1/2 teaspoon black pepper
Green peppers, chopped, to garnish
Cucumbers, chopped, to garnish
Croutons, to garnish

Beat together oil and lemon juice. Stir in tomato juice, tomatoes, broth, onions, celery, Tabasco sauce, salt, and pepper. Check seasonings to taste and chill.
Add chopped green peppers, cucumbers, and croutons before serving.

Cherry Soup

6 SERVINGS

3 cups cold water
1 cup sugar
1 cinnamon stick
4 cups sour cherries, pitted and drained
1 tablespoon cornstarch
¼ cup heavy cream
¾ cup dry red wine

Bring water, sugar, and cinnamon stick to boil. Add cherries, partially cover, and simmer for 10 minutes. Remove cinnamon stick.

Mix cornstarch with 2 tablespoons water and add to soup. Bring almost to boil, stirring constantly. Reduce heat and simmer for 2 minutes. Refrigerate.

Before serving, add cream and wine and serve in chilled bowls.

Strawberry Soup

6 SERVINGS

2 cups strawberries
⅓ cup sugar
½ cup sour cream
½ cup red wine
2 cups ice water

Place all but 6 strawberries in blender with sugar, sour cream, and wine. Blend for 1 minute. Add ice water and blend for 2 seconds. Chill in refrigerator overnight. Garnish individual soup bowls with remaining strawberries to serve.

Raspberry Soup

4 SERVINGS

2 cups raspberries
1 cup orange juice
¾ cup white grape juice or weak herb tea
2 tablespoons cornstarch
2 tablespoons red currant jelly
1 tablespoon orange rind, grated
½ cup plain yogurt

Combine raspberries and orange juice in blender or food processor and puree. Rub through fine strainer and transfer to saucepan.

Add grape juice or tea. Mix jelly with cornstarch and add to mixture. Heat to simmer over moderate heat; continue to simmer for 10 minutes. Stir in orange rind and yogurt. Chill before serving.

Melon with Ginger Sauce

8 SERVINGS

1 8-ounce package cream cheese, whipped
5 slices prosciutto ham, diced
½ teaspoon ground ginger
Half-and-half cream, to thin
1 ripe cantaloupe
1 ripe honeydew melon

Put cream cheese, diced ham, and ginger into food processor or blender and process to smooth paste. With machine running, add half-and-half until mixture is thin enough to pour, but is the consistency of lightly whipped cream.

Halve, seed, and peel melons. Slice melons into 24 or more thin wedges each. Arrange melon slices on flat plate, alternating cantaloupe and honeydew, and drizzle with sauce. Serve cool, not cold.

Orange and Carrot Soup

4 SERVINGS

½ cup onion, chopped
3 tablespoons butter
16 small carrots, thinly sliced
2 cups water
1½ cups orange juice
Salt and pepper, to taste
1 cup light cream
Dash of nutmeg
Chives, finely chopped to garnish

Combine all ingredients except cream, nutmeg and chives. Cook until carrots are tender. Puree mixture in blender, or mash through a sieve. If too thick, thin with additional orange juice to desired consistency. Chill.

Before serving, stir in light cream, and season with dash of nutmeg. Garnish with finely chopped chives.

Chinese Chicken Soup

6 SERVINGS

4 to 5 spring onions
5 cups strongly-flavored, clear chicken stock
6 small mushrooms, finely sliced and sautéed
2 cups shredded white chicken meat
2 eggs
Pepper, to taste
2 to 3 teaspoons soy sauce

Finely slice white part of spring onions, reserving green part for garnish. Heat chicken stock until boiling. Add sautéed mushrooms, onions, and shredded white chicken meat.

Beat eggs until frothy; season with pepper. Stir soup well. Pour beaten eggs steadily into soup, stirring constantly, so that eggs remain in shreds. Allow to cook for one or two minutes to set the eggs. Add soy sauce and season to taste.

Serve in soup bowls sprinkled with the finely chopped green parts of the spring onions.

Broiled Chicken Wings

4 SERVINGS

1 pound chicken wings
3 tablespoons soy sauce
3 tablespoons lemon juice
1/8 teaspoon onion powder
1 tablespoon honey
1 tablespoon catsup
Salt and pepper, to taste

Cut off outer wing tip. Divide each wing into two parts at joint and put in bowl. Mix together soy sauce, lemon juice, and onion powder and pour over chicken. Cover loosely and marinate in refrigerator several hours or overnight.

When ready to cook, set on highest rack position of pre-heated broiler. Mix honey and catsup with 1 tablespoon marinade and brush on wings. Sprinkle with salt and pepper and broil for 12 minutes.

Salmon Ball

16 SERVINGS

1 16-ounce can red salmon
1 8-ounce package cream cheese
1 tablespoon lemon juice
1 teaspoon lemon rind, grated
1 teaspoon horseradish
1/4 teaspoon salt
1/4 teaspoon liquid smoke
3 tablespoons fresh parsley, snipped
1/2 cup pecans, chopped
Garnish:
1/2 cup parsley flakes
1/2 cup walnuts, finely chopped

Drain and flake salmon. Combine all ingredients except garnish and chill overnight. Shape into ball. Roll in parsley and nuts.

Cheese Apple

8 SERVINGS

1/4 pound cream cheese, softened
1/4 pound American cheese, grated
1/4 onion, grated
1 tablespoon catsup
1/4 teaspoon salt
2 tablespoons parsley, chopped
1 teaspoon Worcestershire sauce
Dash of garlic powder
Paprika, to garnish

Mix together all ingredients, except paprika. Place in refrigerator overnight. Form into apple shape. Cover with paprika, adding sprig of parsley for stem.

Marinated Mushrooms

4 SERVINGS

1 pound mushrooms
1 cup wine vinegar
1 teaspoon olive oil
1 clove garlic, chopped
1 teaspoon margarine
1/2 teaspoon sage
2 teaspoons parsley or chives, chopped

Remove stems and wipe mushrooms with damp cloth. Leave whole or cut in half if large, if desired. Place in bowl with remaining ingredients. Marinate 12 to 48 hours, stirring occasionally. Drain and serve with toothpicks.

Pickled Herring

6 SERVINGS

2 salt herrings
3/4 cup vinegar
3/4 cup water
2 1/2 teaspoons sugar
1 onion, sliced
Seasonings, to taste

Soak herring overnight. Simmer for 2 minutes with vinegar, water, and sugar. Set aside to cool before using. Sprinkle selected mixed seasonings in bottom of a storage jar. Add sliced onion, then herring. Repeat layers until all herring is used. Pour cooled vinegar mixture on top and refrigerate.

Jellied Gazpacho

Jellied Gazpacho

7 SERVINGS

1 46-ounce can tomato juice
2 envelopes unflavored gelatin
4 tomatoes, peeled, seeded, and chopped
1 cucumber, peeled, seeded, and chopped
½ green pepper, seeded and diced
¼ cup grated onion
4 tablespoons olive oil
4 tablespoons wine vinegar
1 garlic clove, crushed
6 to 8 drops hot pepper sauce
Salt and freshly ground black pepper, to taste

Heat tomato juice, add gelatin, stir until dissolved, and set aside to cool.

Combine tomatoes, cucumber, green pepper, and onion, and add to tomato juice.

Stir in oil and vinegar. Add garlic, hot pepper sauce, salt, and black pepper to taste. Mix well and chill thoroughly, preferably overnight.

Serve in small bowls set in a bed of crushed ice.

Peaches Filled with Cheese

Peaches Filled with Cheese

4 SERVINGS

1 30-ounce can peach halves
3 tablespoons grated cheddar cheese
1 tablespoon grated Parmesan cheese
1 tablespoon softened butter
Salt and cayenne pepper, to taste
Lettuce, to garnish
1 3-ounce package cream cheese
5 to 6 tablespoons light cream
Paprika, to garnish

Drain peaches. Mix cheeses with butter, season to taste with salt and cayenne pepper, and fill peach halves. Arrange on a bed of lettuce on large platter or on individual dishes.

Beat cream cheese and light cream together. Spoon mixture over peaches. Sprinkle with paprika.

VEGETABLES & SALADS

Barbecued Corn

4 SERVINGS

4 - 6 ears fresh corn
Softened butter, to spread
Salt and pepper, to taste

Remove husk and silk from corn and spread generously with softened butter.

Sprinkle with salt and pepper and wrap each cob in double thickness of foil. Twist the ends to seal.

Place corn on barbecue rack over hot coals and cook for approximately 30 minutes, turning frequently.

Barbecued Corn

Marinated Raw Vegetable Salad

12 SERVINGS

Dressing:
2 cups vegetable oil
1 cup white vinegar
1/2 cup lemon juice
Salt, to taste
1 teaspoon oregano leaves
1 teaspoon dry mustard
1 teaspoon garlic powder
1/2 teaspoon anise seed
Salad:
8 small zucchini
4 small yellow squash
1 head broccoli
1 head cauliflower
4 small carrots
2 red onions
1/2 to 1 pound fresh mushrooms

Combine dressing ingredients in large jar. Shake well to mix thoroughly.
Wash and peel vegetables, as desired. Slice all vegetables and combine. Pour dressing over vegetables several hours before serving, stirring occasionally.

Caesar Salad

8 SERVINGS

2 heads romaine lettuce
4 cloves garlic
4 anchovy fillets
Dressing:
1/4 teaspoon pepper
Pinch of salt
1/2 teaspoon dry mustard
1 cup olive oil
1/4 cup vinegar
1/4 cup lemon juice
Garnish:
Croutons
1/2 cup Parmesan cheese, grated
2 coddled eggs

Tear lettuce and put in large bowl. In small bowl, mash anchovies with garlic. Add dressing ingredients to anchovy-garlic mixture. Blend well and pour over greens.
Add croutons, grated cheese, and coddled eggs. Toss gently before serving.

Curried Crab Salad

2 SERVINGS

8 ounces backfin crab meat, cartilage removed
1/2 cup mushrooms, thinly sliced
1/4 cup green pepper, diced
1 tablespoon lemon juice
Freshly ground black pepper, to taste
1/4 cup plain yogurt
2 teaspoons mayonnaise
1/2 to 3/4 teaspoon curry powder
1 tablespoon parsley, minced
1 tablespoon scallion tops, minced
1 medium tomato, cut in wedges, to garnish
1/2 cucumber, sliced, to garnish
Lemon wedges, to garnish

Combine crabmeat, mushrooms, green pepper, lemon juice, pepper, yogurt, mayonnaise, curry powder, parsley, and scallion tops. Chill for 1 hour.
Spoon onto chilled serving plates and garnish with tomato, cucumber, and lemon wedges.

Mexican Salad

8 SERVINGS

Dressing:
1/2 cup mayonnaise
1/2 cup sour cream
1/2 cup green onions, chopped
1/2 cup parsley, chopped
1 tablespoon lemon juice
1 teaspoon dill
1 teaspoon salt
1 teaspoon sugar
Salad:
2 medium zucchini, thinly sliced
2 medium yellow squash, thinly sliced
1 16-ounce can red kidney beans, drained
1/2 pound mushrooms, thinly sliced
2 cups lettuce, shredded
Radish slices, to garnish
Dill, to garnish

Stir together dressing ingredients. Set aside. In 2-quart glass bowl, place zucchini and yellow squash in one layer, top with 1/4 of mayonnaise mixture. Repeat layering with remaining vegetables and dressing.
Cover and chill for at least 4 hours.
To serve, garnish with radish slices and dill.

Spinach and Cabbage Salad

6 SERVINGS

2 cups cabbage, finely shredded
2 cups raw spinach leaves, washed and shredded
2 cups celery, chopped
Dressing:
1/2 cup salad oil
2 tablespoons vinegar
1 tablespoon catsup
1/2 teaspoon salt
1/2 teaspoon paprika
1/8 teaspoon pepper
1/4 teaspoon celery seed
1 clove garlic, crushed

Combine cabbage, spinach, and celery. Mix dressing ingredients, stirring or shaking well. Toss with combined greens and serve.

Cabbage Salad

4 SERVINGS

2 large onions
1 large carrot
1 pepper
1 cucumber
2 cups cabbage, shredded
3 tablespoons vinegar
3 tablespoons oil
3 tablespoons sugar
1 tablespoon salt

Thinly slice onions, carrot, pepper, and cucumber. Combine with cabbage in large bowl. Mix together vinegar, oil, sugar, and salt. Pour over vegetables. Cover tightly. Marinate for 2 days.

Marinated Carrot Salad

4 SERVINGS

5 carrots, peeled and sliced
3 tablespoons olive oil
1/2 cup vinegar
2 pinches of black pepper
5 sprigs parsley, chopped
1 teaspoon garlic powder

Boil or steam carrots until just tender. Drain and let cool. Mix together olive oil, vinegar, black pepper, parsley, and garlic powder. Add carrots and marinate for 24 hours.

Chicken-Pineapple Salad

6 SERVINGS

3 fresh pineapples
3 cups cooked chicken, cubed
1/2 cup almonds, lightly toasted and slivered
1/2 cup sour cream
Salt and pepper, to taste
1/2 cup mayonnaise
1/2 cup coconut, freshly grated, to garnish

Cut pineapples in half lengthwise. Do not remove stalks. Hollow each half, leaving about 1/2 inch of shell and fruit.
Reserve fruit and mince. Blend sour cream into mayonnaise. Season to taste.
Toss ingredients gently. Fill pineapple shells with mixture, and top with freshly grated coconut.

Macaroni Salad

6 SERVINGS

1 cup elbow macaroni, cooked
1/3 cup mayonnaise
1 tablespoon lemon juice
1 cup raw turnip, finely grated
2 tablespoons green onion, chopped
1/2 cup celery, finely diced
1/2 teaspoon salt
1/8 teaspoon pepper
Lettuce leaves, to garnish

Drain cooked macaroni, rinse with cold water, and drain again.
Combine macaroni with mayonnaise, lemon juice, turnip, onion, celery, salt, and pepper in a large bowl. Mix well, cover, and chill thoroughly. Serve on lettuce leaves.

Carrot Salad

8 SERVINGS

7 medium carrots, grated
1/2 cup raisins
1 cup non-fat yogurt
1/4 cup orange juice
1 teaspoon lemon juice

Combine carrots and raisins. Blend 1/2 cup of carrot-raisin mixture with yogurt, orange juice, and lemon juice. Combine this mixture with remaining carrot-raisin mixture and mix well.
Chill to serve cold.

Turkey Salad with Celery, Grapes, and Nuts

Turkey Salad with Celery, Grapes, and Nuts

4 SERVINGS

2 cups chopped turkey
1/2 cup seedless grapes, peeled
1/2 cup sliced celery
3 to 4 tablespoons almonds
1 cup mayonnaise
Juice of 1/2 lemon
Grated rind of 1/2 orange
Lettuce or endive leaves, to garnish
1/2 teaspoon paprika, to garnish

Pre-heat oven to 350°F.
Chop turkey into medium size pieces. Peel grapes after dipping in boiling, then cold, water.
Dip almonds in boiling water, remove skins, and brown halved nuts in 350°F oven for 5 minutes.
Add lemon juice and grated orange rind to mayonnaise. Mix turkey and other ingredients into mayonnaise. Arrange on lettuce or endive leaves and sprinkle with paprika.

California Chicken Salad

4 SERVINGS

2 whole chicken breasts, fried or stewed
2 tablespoons hot water
1 teaspoon dry mustard
1 tablespoon sesame seeds
1/2 teaspoon salt
2 teaspoons sugar
1 cup watercress, chopped
4 to 5 scallions, chopped
20 strands cellophane noodles, fried
1/2 head lettuce, shredded
Italian salad dressing, to taste

Remove skin and bones from chicken breasts and cut meat into small pieces. Set aside. Combine hot water and mustard until mustard forms a paste. Stir into chicken pieces. Add sesame seeds, salt, and sugar and toss. Add watercress, scallions, noodles, and lettuce; toss again. Add Italian dressing to taste and toss one final time.

Rainbow Salad

4 SERVINGS

¼ pound cooked ham, diced
1 cup cottage cheese
Pinch of cayenne pepper
¼ teaspoon salt
1 cucumber
4 ribs celery, chopped
2 red dessert apples, cored and chopped but not peeled
2 carrots, grated
2 tablespoons lemon juice
Lettuce, to garnish
2 hard-boiled eggs, to garnish
Parsley or watercress, to garnish
Dressing:
½ cup yogurt
1 teaspoon lemon juice
Pinch of garlic salt
1 teaspoon prepared mustard
Black pepper, to taste
Paprika, to taste

Combine ham, cottage cheese, pepper, and salt. Thinly slice half of the cucumber. Arrange the thin slices of cucumber around edge of large platter; cut the rest into ¼-inch diced cubes. Put diced cucumber, celery, apples, and carrots into bowl, add lemon juice, and mix well. Arrange on platter, with lettuce leaves in the center and ham and cheese mixture on top.
Cut eggs in half lengthwise and arrange on top. Place sprig of parsley or watercress in center of platter.
To make dressing, combine all ingredients; mix until smooth. Serve over salad.

Rainbow Salad

Frosted Cranberry Salad

4 SERVINGS

1 8-ounce can cranberry sauce
3 tablespoons lemon juice
1 3-ounce package cream cheese, whipped
¼ cup mayonnaise
¼ cup confectioner's sugar, sifted
1 cup walnuts, chopped
1 cup whipping cream
Lettuce leaves, to garnish

Crush cranberry sauce with fork. Add lemon juice. Pour into 8-ounce paper cups. Combine cream cheese, mayonnaise, sugar, and walnuts. Blend well. Fold in whipping cream and spread over cranberry mixture. Freeze until firm.
Before serving, gently tear away paper cups and serve on lettuce leaves.

Asparagus Parmesan

8 SERVINGS

3 pounds fresh asparagus
1 cup dry bread crumbs
1 tablespoon Parmesan cheese, grated
¼ teaspoon garlic powder
1 teaspoon salt
Dash of pepper
1 egg
2 tablespoons white wine
½ cup flour

Remove tough ends of asparagus and wash thoroughly in cold salt water. Mix crumbs with cheese, garlic powder, salt, and pepper. Beat egg with wine and pour into shallow dish. Place flour and crumb mixture in separate dishes. Dip asparagus in flour, then in egg beaten with wine, and coat with crumb mixture. Sauté 10 minutes or until tender.

Salade Niçoise

4 SERVINGS

4 tomatoes, quartered
1/2 onion, sliced
1 green pepper, sliced
8 radishes
2 lettuce hearts
4 stalks celery, sliced
1 8-ounce can tuna
8 anchovy fillets
2 hard-boiled eggs, quartered
8 ripe olives, pitted
Dressing:
2 tablespoons wine vinegar
6 tablespoons oil
Salt and pepper, to taste
12 basil leaves, coarsely chopped

Combine vegetables in bowl, placing tuna fish, anchovies, and eggs on top. Dot with olives. Combine ingredients for dressing and pour over salad.

Mixed Vegetables with Water Chestnuts

6 SERVINGS

1 pound green beans
1 pound carrots, sliced
16-ounce can water chestnuts
1/4 cup vegetable oil
2/3 cup vinegar
Garnish:
Lettuce leaves
4 stalks celery, sliced
1/4 cup black or green olives, sliced

Cook vegetables to desired tenderness and drain, set aside to cool. Quarter water chestnuts and combine with cooled vegetables. Mix together oil and vinegar and pour over vegetables. Cover and marinate in refrigerator for several hours or overnight. Drain. Arrange on lettuce leaves, and top with celery and olives to serve.

Zucchini Salad

6 SERVINGS

6 zucchini squash, scrubbed but unpeeled
1 onion, sliced
1 clove garlic, sliced
French dressing, to taste

Lettuce leaves, to garnish
Tomatoes, sliced, to garnish
Parmesan cheese, grated, to garnish

Parboil zucchini in salted water for 6 minutes; drain well. Cut into thick slices and combine with onion and garlic. Cover with French dressing. Marinate overnight.

Drain and discard onion and garlic. Place lettuce leaves on serving platter and arrange on thin slices of overlapping tomato on lettuce leaves. Arrange zucchini on top. Sprinkle with grated Parmesan cheese before serving.

Almond Asparagus

4 SERVINGS

1 pound asparagus
2 tablespoons butter
1 tablespoon lemon juice
1/2 cup almonds, slivered and toasted
Salt and pepper, to taste

Wash asparagus; cut into 1-inch diagonal slices. Heat butter in skillet, add asparagus pieces, and sauté 3 to 4 minutes. Cover and steam for 2 minutes or until tender but crisp.

Toss with lemon juice and almonds. Season to taste with salt and pepper.

German Potato Salad

6 SERVINGS

6 large potatoes
2 large onions, chopped
Dressing:
3 tablespoons sugar
1 tablespoon salt
1/4 teaspoon pepper
1/2 teaspoon dry mustard
1/4 teaspoon paprika
1/2 cup vinegar
1/2 cup salad oil
Parsley, to taste
Celery seed, to taste
Lettuce to garnish

Boil potatoes with skins on. Peel, slice, and add to chopped onions in large bowl.

Mix together remaining ingredients and pour over potatoes and onions.

Toss lightly and serve on bed of lettuce.

FISH & SEAFOOD

Marinated Shrimp

6 SERVINGS

2½ pounds shrimp, cooked and deveined
1 large onion, sliced
8 bay leaves
1½ cup vegetable oil
¾ cup vinegar
2½ tablespoons celery seed
2½ teaspoons capers, with juice
Dash of Tabasco sauce

Place shrimp and onion slices in alternate layers in shallow dish. Add bay leaves.

Combine remaining ingredients and pour over shrimp and onions. Cover and refrigerate at least 48 hours. Remove shrimp from marinade before serving.

Grilled Shrimp in Mustard Sauce

2 SERVINGS

3 tablespoons dry mustard
¼ teaspoon salt
1 teaspoon sugar
1 teaspoon horseradish
¾ cup flat beer
1 pound shrimp, cleaned and deveined
4 tablespoons butter, melted
Prepared duck sauce, to garnish

Mix together mustard, salt, sugar, and horseradish. Add enough beer to make smooth paste. Gradually add remainder of beer to thin. Let mixture stand for 1 hour. Add more beer or cold water if mixture becomes too thick.

Dip shrimp in mustard sauce, thread on skewers, and brush with melted butter. Grill for approximately 8 minutes, turning frequently. Serve with duck sauce.

Chinese Halibut

2 SERVINGS

1½ pounds halibut, cut into small chunks
1 tablespoon oil
1 medium onion, chopped
Sauce:
1½ cups water
1 tablespoon oil
Pinch of salt
3 teaspoons soy sauce
Pinch of freshly ground pepper
2 cloves garlic, minced
1 scallion, sliced
1 stalk celery, chopped
1 egg, beaten
2 tablespoons cornstarch dissolved in 3 tablespoons water

Boil halibut in pot of water for 2 minutes. Heat oil in skillet and brown onion. Transfer fish to skillet. Mix together sauce ingredients. Pour sauce on fish, and add garlic, scallion, and celery.

Cover skillet and simmer for 2 minutes. Pour beaten egg slowly into sauce, mixing constantly. Mix cornstarch and water and stir into sauce. Simmer until thickened.

Fish in Green Tomato Sauce

6 SERVINGS

2 tablespoons oil
1 large onion, thinly sliced
2 cans Mexican green tomatoes (tomatillos)
⅓ cup cilantro, minced
1 to 2 small, hot green chiles
2 pounds fresh red snapper or cod
2 cups zucchini, thinly sliced

In 12-inch frying pan, heat oil and sauté onions until transparent. Remove from pan with slotted spoon and set aside. In blender, put green tomatoes, cilantro, and chiles; blend well.

Cut fish into 2-inch pieces and set in frying pan. Distribute onions over fish and pour sauce over all.

Simmer over medium heat for 5 minutes, then gently stir in zucchini. Continue to cook until fish flakes easily with fork, approximately 5 minutes.

Serve over rice with dollop of sour cream.

Crab Meat Kebabs

Crab Meat Kebabs

4 SERVINGS

1 cup bread crumbs
2 tablespoons dry sherry
2 cups crab meat cartilage removed
1 teaspoon dry mustard
1 teaspoon chopped tarragon
Bacon slices, to wrap

Soak bread crumbs in sherry. Combine crab meat, soaked bread crumbs, mustard, and tarragon, and roll into small balls.

Wrap ½ slice bacon around each ball and thread on skewers. Sauté approximately 15 minutes. Serve warm.

Shrimp in Garlic Butter

6 SERVINGS

1 garlic clove, cut in half
½ cup butter or margarine
48 jumbo shrimp, peeled and deveined
3 tablespoons parsley, finely chopped
½ cup sherry

Sauté garlic in butter for 2 minutes. Remove garlic. Add shrimp to butter and sauté for 5 minutes over medium heat or until shrimp are pink. Remove shrimp to hot platter.

Add parsley and sherry to butter in pan. Increase heat and sauté for 30 seconds. Pour sauce over shrimp and serve immediately.

Trout with Almonds

6 SERVINGS

6 brook trout
Tarragon, to taste
Salt, to taste
Pepper, to taste
Oil, to taste
¼ cup butter
½ cup blanched, slivered almonds
6 slices bacon
Lemon wedges, to garnish

Season inside of trout with tarragon, teaspoon butter for each trout, butter, salt, and pepper. Rub outside of fish with oil. Cook on barbecue rack for approximately 15 minutes, turning once.

While trout is grilling, sauté almonds in remaining butter until butter foams and nuts are golden brown.

Place bacon on barbecue rack for approximately 5 minutes before fish is done.

To serve, pour foaming butter and almonds over trout, and serve with lemon wedges and bacon slices.

Trout with Almonds

Pasta Salad with Salmon

8 SERVINGS

2 cups macaroni shells
½ cup celery, chopped
½ cup carrot, grated
¼ cup green pepper, chopped
1 teaspoon dill
1 teaspoon dried onion, minced
1 7-ounce can salmon, drained and flaked
½ cup mayonnaise
½ cup sour cream
Salt and pepper, to taste

Cook and drain shells. Combine with celery, carrot, green pepper, dill, onion and salmon. Blend mayonnaise and sour cream in a small bowl until smooth. Add to macaroni-salmon mixture. Season with salt and pepper.

Press into greased 4-cup mold. Chill for 2 hours.

Seafood in White Wine

12 SERVINGS

10 tablespoons butter
⅔ cup flour
1 teaspoon paprika
2 teaspoons salt
¼ teaspoon white pepper
3 cups light cream
1¼ cups dry white wine
4 8-ounce rock lobster tails
2 pounds jumbo shrimp, slightly steamed, peeled and
  deveined
2 7½ ounce cans, Alaskan King crab meat, drained

Melt butter in Dutch oven. Stir in flour, paprika, salt, and pepper until smooth. Gradually stir in cream, mixing until smooth. Bring to a boil, stirring constantly. Reduce heat and simmer for 5 minutes.

Add wine, lobster, shrimp, and crab meat. Stir gently until combined. Cook over low heat until heated thoroughly. Serve over white rice.

Tuna Risotto

4 SERVINGS

Risotto:
4 tablespoons oil
½ onion, finely chopped
1½ cups long grain rice
2 cups chicken stock, heated
Sauce:
2 tablespoons oil
2 tablespoons margarine
½ onion, finely chopped
2 tablespoons tomato puree
3 tablespoons wine vinegar
2 tablespoons lemon juice
1 7-ounce can tuna, flaked
Grated cheese, to garnish

To make risotto, heat oil in sauce pan, add onion, and sauté until transparent. Add rice and stir over low heat until golden. Remove from heat, add hot stock, stir, and return to stove. Cover and simmer until rice is tender.

To make sauce, heat oil and margarine in saucepan, add onion, and sauté until soft and golden.

Add tomato puree, vinegar, lemon juice, and flaked tuna. Mix well and heat thoroughly. Season to taste.

Stir into the risotto just before serving, sprinkling with a little grated cheese. Serve extra cheese separately.

Fillets of Sole with Vegetables

2 SERVINGS

1 rib celery, thinly sliced
1 scallion, thinly sliced
2 carrots, thinly sliced
1 tablespoon butter
¾ cup heavy cream
½ teaspoon salt
2 fillets of sole, approximately 1 pound

Sauté celery, scallion and carrots in butter until vegetables are tender. Stir in cream and salt. Add sole fillets, cover and simmer for 5 to 10 minutes, or until sole is opaque.

Remove sole to serving plate and simmer sauce for 5 minutes longer. To serve, pour sauce over sole on serving plate.

MEATS

Grilled Hamburgers with Vegetables

4 SERVINGS

4 hamburger patties
2 medium potatoes, sliced
1 large onion, sliced
2 medium carrots, scraped and sliced
2 tablespoons bacon, cooked and diced
4 pats of butter
Salt and pepper, to taste

Lay out 4 sheets of heavy-duty aluminum foil, 24 inches by 18 inches each. Fold sheets to double thickness. Place 1 hamburger patty on each sheet.
Divide potatoes, onion, carrots, and bacon evenly over hamburgers. Place 1 pat of butter on each; season with salt and pepper. Wrap foil packets, sealing edges tightly with triple folds, but allowing some air space around foods. Place sealed packets in hot coals to bake 16 to 18 minutes, turning once, for medium doneness and tender-crisp vegetables.

Beef Kebabs

4 SERVINGS

1/4 cup Worcestershire sauce
2 tablespoons brown sugar
2 tablespoons lemon juice
2 teaspoons caraway seed
1 teaspoon onion powder
1 teaspoon salt
1/2 teaspoon garlic powder
1 1/2 pounds lean beef cubes, cut into 1-inch pieces

Combine all ingredients except beef cubes; mix well. Place beef cubes in snug-fitting bowl or plastic bag. Pour marinade over meat. Cover and marinate for 4 to 6 hours.
Arrange beef cubes on skewers. Grill over hot charcoal or place on rack in pre-heated broiler for 5 to 10 minutes, turning and brushing with marinade several times.

Veal Scallopini

4 SERVINGS

1 1/2 pounds veal cutlets
1/3 cup flour
1 teaspoon salt
1/4 teaspoon pepper
1/3 cup butter or margarine
1/2 green pepper, chopped
1 large onion, chopped
1 garlic clove, minced
1 7-ounce can tomato soup
1/2 cup water
Pinch of oregano
1/2 cup cheese, grated

Cut veal into serving pieces. Roll in mixture of flour, salt, and pepper. Heat butter or margarine in large skillet. Sauté green pepper, onion, and garlic until tender. Remove from pan and set aside. Add veal cutlets and brown on both sides. Pour off excess fat.
Return cutlets to skillet. Add soup, water, and oregano to veal cutlets. Stir in reserved onion and green pepper.
Cover and simmer until tender, approximately 15 minutes. Sprinkle with cheese and heat until cheese is melted.

Chili Con Carne

8 SERVINGS

1 pound ground steak
1 cup onions, chopped
1 cup celery, diced
2 cups canned tomatoes
1 teaspoon salt
3 teaspoons chili powder
1 2 pound, 8 ounce-can kidney beans
1 cup tomato juice

Sauté ground steak until slightly brown. Add onions and celery. Sauté mixture, stirring constantly, for 3 minutes. Add tomatoes, salt, and chili powder and simmer for 30 minutes, stirring frequently, to avoid sticking.
Add kidney beans and tomato juice and simmer another 10 minutes, stirring occasionally.

Home Sweet Home

Turkey Cottage Pie

4 SERVINGS

1 pound potatoes
3 onions, 1 peeled, 2 chopped
6 tablespoons butter
1/2 cup milk
2 slices bacon, chopped
1/2 cup chopped mushrooms
1/2 cup turkey stock
1 tablespoon chopped parsley
1 tablespoon chopped tarragon
3 cups turkey, diced
1/8 teaspoon mace
Salt and pepper, to taste

Pre-heat oven to 400°F.

Peel potatoes, place in saucepan with peeled onion and cover with salted water. Bring to a boil and cook 15 to 20 minutes. While potatoes boil, sauté chopped onions in 3 tablespoons butter until transparent. Add chopped bacon pieces and sauté for 3 minutes. Add chopped mushrooms and sauté for 5 minutes longer.

Stir in stock and chopped herbs and season to taste with salt and pepper. Bring mixture to a boil, simmer for 3 minutes, then stir in diced turkey. Pour mixture into an ovenproof dish.

Remove onion and drain potatoes. Mash potatoes, add butter and milk, mixing thoroughly. Stir in mace and season to taste with salt and pepper.

Spread mashed potatoes carefully all over top of casserole in a smooth layer. Bake for 30 minutes, or until potato topping is golden brown and crisp.

American Country Life

Braised Veal with Lemon

6 SERVINGS

2½ pounds boneless veal, cut in 1½-inch pieces
Flour, to dredge
3 tablespoons butter
Juice of 2 lemons
⅔ cup dry white wine
Salt and pepper, to taste
½ cup parsley, minced

Coat meat with flour and shake off excess. Brown veal in butter, stirring constantly. Stir in lemon juice. Simmer covered, shaking pan frequently, for 3 minutes. Stir in wine. Season with salt and pepper. Simmer, covered, for 15 to 20 minutes or until tender. Before serving, sprinkle with parsley.

Country Supper

4 SERVINGS

3 tablespoons vegetable oil
4 large potatoes, thinly sliced
3 large carrots, sliced
½ cup celery, sliced
1 medium onion, chopped
Salt and pepper, to taste
1 pound smoked sausage

Sauté potatoes, carrots, celery and onions in oil over low heat in a heavy skillet. Season to taste.
When potatoes and carrots are tender, place sausage on top. Cover and cook over low heat for 12 minutes, or until sausage is thoroughly cooked.

Orange-Glazed Pork Chops

2 SERVINGS

1 teaspoon vegetable oil
2 ½-inch thick pork chops
Salt and pepper, to taste,
1 tablespoon yellow onion, finely chopped
¼ cup water
1 tablespoon orange juice
1 medium sweet potato, peeled and cut into ¼-inch
  circles

Heat oil in heavy skillet to almost smoking. Sprinkle pork chops with salt and pepper. Sear quickly in hot oil, turning twice, about 3 minutes per side.
Remove pork chops to warm platter. Reduce heat

under skillet and add onion. Sauté for 1 minute, then stir in water and orange juice. Add sweet potato circles. Bring to a simmer and cook, covered, for 15 minutes.
Place pork chops on vegetables, cover pan and cook 10 to 15 minutes longer or until pork is no longer pink. Add water if necessary.
To serve, place pork chops on serving platter, surrounded by vegetables.

Veal Steak

4 SERVINGS

1 garlic clove, halved
4 veal shoulder steaks
4 tablespoons butter
Salt and pepper, to taste
1 tablespoon fresh parsley, chopped
1 tablespoon tomato paste
¼ cup warm water
½ cup dry red wine or water

Rub both sides of veal steaks with garlic cloves.
Melt butter in heavy skillet and sauté steaks until well-browned on both sides.
Mix salt and pepper, parsley, tomato paste and water together and stir in wine or water. Pour over veal steaks and simmer for 5 minutes or until meat is tender and sauce has thickened.

Spicy Beef Sauté

4 SERVINGS

¼ cup teriyaki sauce
¼ cup red wine or water
1 tablespoon red wine vinegar
1 pound beef round steak
2 tablespoons vegetable oil
2 garlic cloves, minced
2 teaspoons cayenne
⅛ teaspoon anise seed

Combine teriyaki sauce, red wine or water and vinegar. Set aside.
Cut beef into ⅛-inch strips.
Heat vegetable oil in a large skillet over medium heat.
Add garlic, cayenne and anise seeds and sauté for 30 seconds.
Add beef strips and sauté until just browned.
Pour teriyaki mixture over beef. Simmer 5 minutes, uncovered, or until sauce thickens.
Serve over hot rice.

POULTRY

Chicken in White Wine

4 SERVINGS

4 chicken breasts
1/4 cup flour
1 teaspoon garlic salt
1/4 teaspoon pepper
1/2 teaspoon thyme
8 tablespoons butter
1 cup white wine
1/4 cup onions, sliced
8 mushrooms, sliced
2 tablespoons parsley, finely minced

Shake chicken parts in brown paper bag containing flour, garlic salt, pepper, and thyme. Melt 6 tablespoons butter in heavy skillet and brown chicken well on all sides.

Pour wine over chicken, cover tightly, and simmer for 20 minutes. While chicken simmers, sauté onion and mushrooms in remaining 2 tablespoons butter in small skillet until tender. Add to chicken at end of 20 minutes, cover, and cook 15 minutes longer.

Garnish with parsley to serve.

Chicken Fricassee with Meat Balls

8 SERVINGS

2 onions, chopped
1 rib celery, chopped
1 green pepper, chopped
2 tablespoons margarine
1/2 teaspoon salt
1/2 teaspoon onion salt
1/2 teaspoon black or red pepper
1/2 teaspoon garlic salt
1 teaspoon paprika
1 pound ground beef
1/4 teaspoon garlic powder

1 onion, minced
1 chicken, cut up

Sauté chopped celery, onions, and green pepper in margarine until onions are transparent. Season with 1/4 teaspoon each salt, pepper, and garlic salt.

Coat chicken with 1/2 teaspoon paprika. Use enough paprika to coat mixture red; set aside.

Season meat with remaining salt, onion salt, pepper, garlic salt and powder, and paprika. Add minced onion, mix, and form into meat balls.

Place meat balls on onion mixture; place chicken on meat balls. Add water to cover only meat balls. Bring to boil and simmer, covered, on low heat for 2 hours. Flavor is enhanced if prepared ahead and reheated before serving.

Country Chicken

4 SERVINGS

1/4 cup flour
1 teaspoon salt
1/8 teaspoon pepper
1/4 teaspoon oregano, crushed
4 chicken breasts
4 chicken wings
3 tablespoons butter
3/4 cup white wine
1 tablespoon lemon juice
1/2 cup onion, chopped
1 cup mushrooms, sliced
2 medium tomatoes, peeled and diced
1 teaspoon sugar
1/4 cup water

Blend together flour, salt, pepper, and oregano. Set aside 1 tablespoon of flour mixture. Coat chicken with remaining flour mixture and brown chicken in 2 tablespoons butter. Combine wine and lemon juice and pour over chicken. Add onion. Bring to a boil, reduce heat and simmer, covered, for 45 minutes or until tender. Remove chicken to platter and keep warm.

In small skillet, sauté mushrooms in 1 tablespoon butter until tender. Drain.

Mix mushrooms, tomatoes, and sugar into chicken sauce. Cook until vegetables are tender, approximately 5 minutes.

Blend together reserved flour and water; add to sauce. Stir over medium heat until thick and bubbly. Pour over chicken before serving.

The Wayside Inn

Chicken in Soy Sauce

6 SERVINGS

2 pounds chicken pieces
1 teaspoon garlic salt
1 teaspoon paprika
¼ teaspoon black pepper
2 tablespooons vegetable oil
1 large onion, sliced
1½ large green peppers, cut in thin strips
1 cup celery, sliced
1¼ cups chicken broth
2 tablespoons cornstarch
3 tablespoons soy sauce
2 large tomatoes, cut in eighths
3 cups hot cooked rice

Skin and bone chicken. Cut meat in thin strips. Sprinkle with seasonings.

Sauté chicken in oil 1 to 2 minutes. Add onion, green peppers, celery, and broth. Cover; steam for 2 minutes.

Blend cornstarch and soy sauce. Stir into chicken mixture. Add tomatoes; cook and stir for 2 minutes or until sauce is slightly thickened.

Serve over rice.

Turkey Croquettes

4 SERVINGS

3 tablespoons butter
3 tablespoons flour
1 cup half-and-half cream
Salt and pepper, to taste
2 cups cooked turkey, ground
2 tablespoons parsley, chopped
2 teaspoons lemon juice
2 teaspoons Worcestershire sauce
1 egg, beaten
Fine bread crumbs, to dredge
Fat, to deep fry

Melt butter over low heat, stirring in flour. Whisk in cream, stirring constantly until mixture thickens. Season to taste with salt and pepper. Add turkey, parsley, lemon juice, and Worcestershire sauce.
Spread mixture in 9-inch greased pan to 1-inch thickness. Chill. Cut into bars and mold into croquettes. Chill again.
Dip croquettes into egg, then in bread crumbs. Chill again. Fry in deep fat until golden brown, approximately 3 or 4 minutes. Serve plain or with cream sauce.

Stir-Fry Chicken with Vegetables

6 SERVINGS

1 teaspoon salt
2 tablespoons sherry
2 teaspoons cornstarch
1/8 teaspoon pepper
1/2 pound chicken cutlets, cut in 1-inch pieces
3 tablespoons oil
1 green pepper, cubed
1 cup mushrooms, cubed

Mix together salt, sherry, cornstarch, and pepper to make marinade. Add chicken and marinate for 10 minutes.
Heat 1 tablespoon oil in wok. Add green pepper and mushrooms and stir-fry for 2 minutes. Remove from wok.
Heat 2 tablespoons oil in wok. Add marinated chicken and stir-fry until opaque. Add reserved vegetables and stir-fry 1 minute. Add 1 tablespoon water if mixture is too dry.
Serve immediately.

Grilled Turkey Breast

8 SERVINGS

2 to 4 pounds fresh turkey breast halves
Sauce:
1/4 cup butter, melted
1/3 cup honey
1 tablespoon Dijon-style mustard
1 teaspoon curry powder
1/4 teaspoon garlic powder

Using indirect heating with covered, kettle-type grill, cook turkey over hot coals to an internal temperature of 170 to 175° F (2 to 4 pounds, approximately 1½ to 2 hours; 4 to 5 pounds, approximately 2 to 2½ hours). Check for doneness 15 minutes before minimum time given.
Combine sauce ingredients; brush turkey with sauce frequently during last 30 minutes of grilling. Brush again before serving.

Chicken Tarragon

4 SERVINGS

1½ tablespoons butter
4 large chicken breasts, halved
1 medium onion, finely chopped
1 large garlic clove, peeled and minced
2 tablespoons fresh parsley, chopped
1½ tablespoons fresh chives, chopped
2 teaspoons dried tarragon leaves
1/2 cup dry white wine
1½ teaspoons lemon juice
1/2 teaspoon salt
1/8 teaspoon freshly ground black pepper

Melt butter in large, heavy, deep-sided skillet over medium-high heat. Add chicken breasts and brown lightly on all sides. Add onion, garlic, and parsley, stirring for 3 to 4 minutes, or until onion is transparent.
Stir in remaining ingredients and bring to a boil. Lower heat and simmer, covered, for 20 minutes. Remove cover and simmer 20 to 25 minutes longer or until chicken is just tender and most of liquid has evaporated from skillet.
Spoon remaining pan juices over each chicken breast and serve.

DESSERTS

Chocolate-Orange Mousse

2 SERVINGS

½ teaspoon orange rind, grated
2 tablespoons light brown sugar, firmly packed
1 egg plus 1 egg yolk
3 squares (3 ounces) semi-sweet chocolate, melted and
    cooled
1½ tablespoons orange juice
½ cup whipping cream

Combine orange rind, sugar, egg yolk, and egg in blender or food processor; whirl until light and foamy. Add chocolate, orange juice, and whipping cream and mix until well-blended.

Pour into individual dessert dishes; chill for 1 hour or until set.

Black Bottoms

48 CUPCAKES

8 ounces cream cheese, softened
1 egg
⅓ cup sugar
Pinch of salt
1 cup chocolate chips
1½ cups flour
1 cup sugar
¼ cup cocoa
¼ teaspoon salt
1 teaspoon baking soda
1 cup water
⅓ cup oil
1 tablespoon vinegar
1 teaspoon vanilla

Pre-heat oven to 350°F.

In small bowl, beat together cream cheese, egg, sugar, and salt. Stir in chocolate chips and set aside.

In large bowl, sift together flour, sugar, cocoa, salt, and baking soda. Add water, oil, vinegar, and vanilla. Mix well with electric mixer. Fill lined miniature muffin tins ⅓ full with chocolate mixture. Top with teaspoon of cream cheese mixture. Bake for 15 to 20 minutes.

Chocolate Icebox Cake

3 8-INCH CAKE LAYERS

Cake Batter:
3 ounces bitter chocolate
1¼ cups boiling water
2 cups sugar
2 cups flour, sifted
¼ cup butter
3 teaspoons baking powder
2 teaspoons vanilla
¼ teaspoon salt
3 eggs
Frosting:
3 ounces bitter chocolate
½ cup butter
1 pound confectioner's sugar
1 egg
1 teaspoon coffee
2 teaspoons vanilla
Salt, to taste
2 to 4 tablespoons milk or cream

Melt chocolate in boiling water and pour over sugar, flour, and butter. Stir until smooth. Refrigerate 8 hours or more.

Pre-heat oven to 350°F.

Add baking powder, vanilla, salt, and eggs to refrigerated mixture. Beat for 2 minutes. Bake in 3 8-inch layer pans for 30 minutes.

To make frosting, melt chocolate and butter together. Beat in remaining ingredients adding enough milk or cream for desired consistency.

Walnut-Peach Pie

1 9-INCH PIE

1 9-inch pie shell, baked
4 cups peaches, peeled and sliced
2 eggs
⅓ cup honey
2 tablespoons butter
½ cup walnuts, coarsely chopped
¼ teaspoon cinnamon

Pre-heat oven to 325°F.

Fill pie shell with peaches. Beat eggs with honey and pour over fruit. Dot with butter, cover with nuts, and sprinkle with cinnamon.

Bake for 35 to 40 minutes until filling is set. Cool before cutting.

Bananas in Rum Sauce

4 SERVINGS

4 tablespoons butter or margarine
2 tablespoons brown sugar
1 teaspoon cinnamon
6 peeled ripe bananas, cut in half lengthwise
¼ cup rum
Vanilla ice cream, if desired

Melt butter in medium skillet.

Mix together brown sugar and cinnamon; sprinkle some over bananas. Sauté bananas in butter over moderate to low heat until lightly browned, turning once. Sprinkle with remaining sugar mixture. Spoon rum over bananas. Serve alone or over vanilla ice cream.

For bananas flambé, heat rum, pour over bananas, and ignite.

Key Lime Pie

1 9-INCH PIE

1 tablespoon unflavored gelatin
1 cup sugar
¼ teaspoon salt
4 eggs, separated
½ cup lime juice
¼ cup water
1 teaspoon lime rind, grated
Green food coloring
1 cup whipping cream, whipped
1 9-inch pie shell, baked

Mix gelatin, ½ cup sugar, and salt in saucepan. Beat together egg yolks, lime juice, and water; stir into gelatin mixture. Bring to a boil over medium heat, stirring constantly. Remove from heat; stir in grated rind. Add enough green food coloring for pale green color. Chill, stirring occasionally, until thickened.

Beat egg whites until soft peaks form. Add remaining sugar gradually, beating until stiff peaks form. Fold gelatin mixture into egg whites. Fold in whipped cream.

Spoon into baked pie shell and chill until firm.

To serve, top with additional whipped cream; and sprinkle additional grated lime rind around edge of pie.

Mocha Parfait

4 SERVINGS

2 bananas
Juice of 1 lemon
16 walnut halves
½ cup cold whipping cream
½ teaspoon vanilla
2 tablespoons sugar
1½ pints coffee ice cream
Bitter chocolate curls, to garnish

Peel bananas, slice, and dip in lemon juice. Divide bananas among 4 parfait glasses. Top each with 4 walnut halves. Chill glasses while whipping cream.

Pour whipping cream into small mixing bowl. Add vanilla; whip until stiff, gradually adding sugar while whipping.

To serve, cube ice cream. Divide among prepared parfait glasses. Top with whipped cream and chocolate curls.

Chocolate Pie

1 9-INCH PIE

4 squares semi-sweet chocolate
2 tablespoons sugar
2 tablespoons water
4 eggs, separated
1 teaspoon vanilla
1 9-inch pie shell, baked
Whipped Cream Topping:
½ pint whipping cream
2 tablespoons confectioner's sugar
Shaved chocolate, to garnish

Stir together chocolate, sugar, and water and heat in double boiler until dissolved. Put in bowl. Add 1 egg yolk at a time, beating after each. Add vanilla. Beat egg whites until stiff. Fold in chocolate mixture. Put in baked pie shell. Refrigerate for several hours.

To make whipped cream topping, chill bowl and beaters. Beat cream until it starts to thicken. Add sugar and beat until stiff. Spread on pie. Top with shaved chocolate.

German Butter Cake

1 13 × 9 × 2-INCH CAKE

5 teaspoons granulated yeast
½ cup sugar
½ cup lukewarm water
½ teaspoon salt
½ cup unsalted butter
¾ cup milk, scalded
Grated rind of 1 lemon
1 teaspoon vanilla
3 large eggs
4 cups flour
Topping:
⅔ cup unsalted butter, softened
¼ cup sugar
¾ cup dark brown sugar
⅔ cup walnuts or pecans, ground
½ teaspoon vanilla
½ teaspoon cinnamon

Pre-heat oven to 375°F. Butter a 13 × 9 × 2-inch baking pan.

Combine yeast with 1 tablespoon sugar in lukewarm water. Allow to foam.

Combine remaining sugar, salt, butter and scalded milk. Cool mixture to lukewarm. Add to yeast.

Add lemon rind, vanilla and eggs, beating well.

Add flour, mixing well. Spread batter into baking pan. Set in a warm place until batter doubles in bulk, about 45 minutes.

To make the topping, cream the butter and sugars. Beat until fluffy. Add remaining topping ingredients and mix well.

Drop by spoonfuls onto the risen dough. Bake for 35 minutes or until top is golden brown.

Cool to serve.

Peace Be to This House

Autumn Fruit

Miniature Fruit Cakes

12 DOZEN CAKES

1 16-ounce bottle maraschino cherries, chopped
6 slices pineapple, chopped
1 cup light brown sugar
1 cup butter
3 eggs
3 cups flour
1/2 cup milk
1 teaspoon vanilla
1 teaspoon baking soda
7 cups pecans, chopped
1 1-pound package chopped dates

Pre-heat oven to 325°F.
Dredge fruit in a small amount of flour. Cream sugar and butter. Add eggs, flour, milk, vanilla and baking soda. Mix well. Fold in pecans, cherries, pineapple and dates. Place 1 tablespoon batter in miniature baking cups, lined with baking cups. Bake for 20 minutes. These fruit cakes can be frozen.

Coffee Dessert

6 SERVINGS

1 1/2 envelopes unflavored gelatin
1 1/2 cups water
1 cup milk
3/4 cup sugar
1/4 teaspoon salt
2 tablespoons instant coffee powder
3 eggs, separated
1 teaspoon vanilla

Combine unflavored gelatin, water, milk, sugar, salt and coffee powder in the top of a double boiler. Stir until the gelatin melts and the mixture begins to simmer.
Add egg yolks and stir until the mixture coats the back of a spoon.
Remove from heat, add vanilla and chill until mixture is the consistency of syrup.
Beat the egg whites until stiff and fold into the chilled mixture. Pour into dessert dishes and chill until firm.

Skillet-Baked Cinnamon Apples

6 SERVINGS

6 baking apples
1/4 cup fine breadcrumbs
2 tablespoons butter, melted
2 tablespoons raisins
2 tablespoons sugar
1 teaspoon cinnamon
1 teaspoon nutmeg
Syrup:
1/3 cup grenadine syrup
1 1/2 cups boiling water
3/4 cup sugar
1 stick cinnamon
2 teaspoons fresh lemon juice

Pre-heat oven to 350°F.

Wash and core apples. Peel a 1-inch strip from top of each apple and arrange in an oven-proof casserole.

Mix breadcrumbs, butter, raisins, sugar, cinnamon and nutmeg. Fill the center of each apple with this mixture.

Combine syrup ingredients in a heavy skillet. When syrup boils, remove from heat and pour over apples. Bake apples 15 to 25 minutes or until apples are tender. Baste several times with syrup.

Remove apples to serving platter and pour syrup over. Serve warm.

Plum Preserve Cookies

24 COOKIES

1/2 cup butter
2/3 cup confectioner's sugar
1 cup flour
Grated zest of 1 lemon
1 1/2 cups plum preserves

Pre-heat oven to 400°F.

Whip butter until light and fluffy. Add confectioner's sugar, flour and lemon zest. Form mixture into 48 tiny round balls.

Place on a lightly oiled cookie sheet. Bake for 5 minutes.

Remove from oven and carefully flatten each round with a glass. Bake for 2 minutes.

Cool cookies on wire rack. When cool, spread 24 cookies with a tablespoon of plum preserves on each. Top with remaining cookies. Sift additional confectioner's sugar over tops of cookies.

Honey Pear Bread

1 9 × 5 × 3-INCH LOAF

2 cups flour, sifted
1 1/2 teaspoons baking powder
1/2 teaspoon baking soda
1/2 teaspoon pumpkin pie spice
1/4 teaspoon salt
1 16-ounce can pears, drained, reserving juice
1/2 cup honey
2 tablespoons vegetable oil
1 egg, beaten
1 teaspoon lemon rind, grated
1/2 cup walnuts, chopped

Pre-heat oven to 350°F.

Sift together flour, baking powder, baking soda and seasonings.

Reserve 2 pear slices and chop remainder finely. Combine chopped pears with honey, oil, egg and lemon rind.

Add to dry ingredients, stirring until mixture is just moistened. Fold in walnuts.

Pour into a greased 9 × 5 × 3-inch loaf pan and bake for 1 hour or until toothpick inserted in middle comes out clean.

Remove from pan and cool before serving. Garnish with pear slices.

Apricot Bread

1 9 × 5 × 3-INCH LOAF

1/3 cup sugar
1 tablespoon flour
1 teaspoon orange rind, grated
1 8-ounce package cream cheese, at room temperature
2 eggs
1/2 cup orange juice
1 17-ounce package apricot-nut quick bread mix

Pre-heat oven to 350°F. Grease and flour 9 × 5 × 3-inch loaf pan.

Combine sugar, flour and orange rind in a small bowl. Add cream cheese and 1 egg. Beat to combine and set mixture aside.

Slightly beat remaining egg, combine with orange juice. Stir in apricot-nut bread mix.

Pour two-thirds bread batter in loaf pan. Spoon cheese mixture evenly over bread batter. Cover with remaining bread mixture.

Bake approximately 1 hour. Remove from oven and cook for 15 minutes. Remove from loaf pan. Serve warm.

Cantaloupe with Ice Cream and Lime Sauce

6 SERVINGS

Lime Sauce:
1/4 cup sugar
2 tablespoons cornstarch
Dash of salt
1/2 cup water
1 tablespoon butter or margarine
1/4 teaspoon fresh lime rind, grated
2 tablespoons fresh lime juice
Fruit:
1 cantaloupe
1 quart vanilla ice cream
1 cup fresh blueberries

To make lime sauce, combine sugar, cornstarch, and salt in small saucepan; stir in water. Cook over medium heat, stirring constantly, until thickened and clear. Remove from heat. Add butter, lime rind, and juice; mix well. Cool.

Cut cantaloupe in half; remove seeds. Slice into 12 equal wedges; remove rind.

Arrange 2 wedges in each individual serving dish. Place 2 scoops vanilla ice cream between melon wedges. Top with blueberries. Pour 2 tablespoons lime sauce over each serving.

Glazed Strawberry Pie

1 9-INCH PIE

2 quarts strawberries
1 9-inch pie shell, baked
1/2 cup water
1 cup sugar
2 1/2 tablespoons cornstarch
1 tablespoon butter
Red food coloring
Whipped cream, to garnish

Wash and drain strawberries and remove stems. Fill baked pie shell with 1 quart or more, as needed, stem end down.

To make strawberry glaze, crush remaining berries and combine with water, sugar, and cornstarch in saucepan. Bring to boil and boil for 2 minutes or until clear. Stir. Add butter and enough food coloring for pleasing color.

Spoon glaze over pie covering all berries. Cool before serving. Decorate rim of pie with whipped cream.

Custard Trifle

4 SERVINGS

1/4 cup sugar
1 tablespoon cornstarch
1/4 teaspoon salt
2 cups milk
2 eggs, slightly beaten
1 teaspoon vanilla
4 cups pound cake, cubed
4 tablespoons brandy
4 tablespoons apricot preserves
1/2 cup whipping cream
1 tablespoon confectioner's sugar
Garnish:
Grated semi-sweet chocolate
Toasted slivered almonds

Combine sugar, cornstarch, and salt in medium saucepan. Stir in milk until well-blended. Bring to boil over medium heat, stirring constantly. Mixture will be thin. Pour mixture in a thin stream into beaten eggs; beat well. Return to saucepan and bring mixture to a slow boil, stirring constantly. Stir in vanilla. Cool mixture covered with waxed paper.

Place cake cubes in glass bowl. Sprinkle with 3 tablespoons of brandy, and drizzle with preserves. Pour custard over cake cubes.

Whip cream with confectioners' sugar until stiff. Fold in 1 tablespoon brandy. Top cake and custard with whipped cream. Garnish with grated chocolate and almonds.

Cover and chill for several hours before serving.

Lemon Sherbet

6 SERVINGS

1 1/2 teaspoons unflavored gelatin
2 tablespoons cold water
2 cups skim milk
3/4 cup sugar
1/2 cup lemon juice
1/2 teaspoon lemon rind, grated
2 egg whites, stiffly beaten

Soak gelatin in water several minutes.

Heat milk. Add sugar and gelatin; stir until dissolved. Chill in refrigerator until just firm. Gradually stir in lemon juice and rind. Pour into freezing tray; freeze to slushy consistency.

Pour into chilled bowl. Beat with electric beater until fluffy but not melted. Fold in egg whites. Return to freezer; freeze until firm.

Autumn in New England—Cider Making

SOUPS & APPETIZERS

Cream of Turkey-Mushroom Soup

8 SERVINGS

¹/₂ pound fresh mushrooms
2 tablespoons unsalted butter
3 cups turkey stock
¹/₂ cup white meat turkey, cooked and chopped
¹/₂ cup heavy cream
Salt and pepper, to taste
Chopped parsley, to garnish

Wash, stem, and slice mushrooms. Sauté in butter until golden brown. Add to turkey stock and simmer, covered, for 5 minutes. Add turkey white meat.

Just before serving, heat cream to simmer. Add to soup. Season to taste and garnish with chopped parsley.

Oyster Chowder

8 SERVINGS

4 strips bacon
2 cups water
1 cup potatoes, diced
1 cup carrots, chopped
1/2 cup onions, diced
1 1/2 cups corn kernels
1 1/2 cups peas
1 cup celery, chopped
2 cups skim milk
1/2 cup fresh parsley, finely chopped
1 teaspoon oregano
1 1/2 teaspoons salt
1/4 teaspoon pepper
2 tablespoons Worcestershire sauce
1/4 cup cornstarch
1 quart small oysters, cut in thirds

Sauté bacon in large saucepan over medium heat until half- done. Drain on paper towels and crumble when cool. Wipe grease from saucepan and add water. Stir in all vegetables and bacon. Cover and simmer until potatoes are tender.

Add 1 cup milk, parsley, spices, and Worcestershire sauce. Pour remaining cup of milk into small bowl. Gradually blend in cornstarch and mix well.

Pour cornstarch mixture into saucepan and stir until well-blended. Add oysters, cover, and simmer for 15 minutes or until oysters curl.

Cheese Puffs

APPROXIMATELY 3 DOZEN

1 cup cheddar cheese, shredded
1 cup margarine
2 cups flour
1 teaspoon salt
Dash of cayenne pepper
1 tablespoon milk
Paprika, to garnish

Pre-heat oven to 350°F.

Combine cheese and margarine. Mix together flour, salt, and pepper and cut into cheese-margarine mixture. Add small amounts of milk to form dough. Chill. Shape into 1-inch balls. Bake for 15 to 20 minutes until puffed. Sprinkle with paprika for color. Dough may be prepared in advance and frozen in plastic bags.

Cucumber Soup

2 SERVINGS

2 small cucumbers
1 tablespoon butter
1 green onion, chopped
1 tablespoon flour
Salt, to taste
1 cup water
1 tablespoon fresh mint leaves, minced
1/2 cup milk
3/4 cup heavy cream, whipped

Peel cucumbers and slice thinly. Reserve several slices as garnish.

Sauté onion in melted butter over low heat until transparent. Add sliced cucumber and simmer until soft.

Stir in flour and salt. Add water and bring to a boil. Simmer for 5 minutes, then strain through a fine sieve until smooth. Stir in mint and chill.

When ready to serve, stir in milk and heavy cream. Garnish with thin slices of cucumber.

Yogurt Soup

6 TO 8 SERVINGS

1 cup barley, cooked
3 tablespoons butter
1 cup onion, finely chopped
4 cups plain yogurt
1 egg
1 tablespoon flour
4 cups chicken broth
1 cup fresh coriander, chopped
Salt and pepper, to taste
Chopped chives, to garnish

Cook barley until tender and set aside. Melt 2 tablespoons butter in a skillet and sauté onions until transparent. Set aside.

Place yogurt in large soup pot over low heat. Gradually stir in egg and flour. Add chicken broth, 1 cup at a time, stirring, until mixture comes to a boil. Add reserved barley and onions and simmer for 30 minutes.

When ready to serve, sauté coriander in 1 tablespoon butter and add to soup. Salt and pepper to taste. Stir well and ladle into hot soup bowls. Garnish with chives.

Vegetable-Cheese Chowder

6 SERVINGS

1/4 cup margarine
1 cup carrots, sliced
1 cup potatoes, cubed
1 cup green beans, sliced
1/2 cup onion, chopped
1/2 cup celery, sliced
1/4 cup green pepper, chopped
3 tablespoons cornstarch
1 teaspoon salt
1 teaspoon dry mustard
4 cups chicken bouillon, cooled
1 tablespoon Worcestershire sauce
1 cup cheddar cheese, coarsely shredded

Melt margarine over medium heat in large saucepan. Add vegetables. Sauté 5 minutes, stirring constantly. Mix together cornstarch, salt, and mustard. Gradually stir in bouillon and Worcestershire sauce until smooth. Add to vegetable mixture.
Bring to boil over medium heat, stirring constantly, and boil 1 minute. Reduce heat, cover, and simmer 30 minutes or until vegetables are tender. Add cheese and stir until melted.

Squash Soup

6 SERVINGS

2 pounds butternut squash
4 cups strong chicken stock
1 large onion, finely chopped
2 medium garlic clove, finely minced
1/4 pound corned beef, finely minced
1/8 teaspoon nutmeg, freshly grated
1/2 teaspoon brown sugar
Salt and freshly ground pepper, to taste

Peel squash. Cut into small, diced pieces, discarding seeds. Combine squash, stock, onion, garlic, and corned beef in large soup pot. Bring to a boil, cover, and simmer over medium heat until squash can be easily pierced with fork, and onions are soft, approximately 12 to 15 minutes.
Cool slightly and add nutmeg and brown sugar. Puree in blender or food processor to a semi-smooth consistency. Return to pot and add salt and pepper to taste. Serve hot.

Crab Pâté

8 SERVINGS

2 8-ounce packages cream cheese, whipped
2 tablespoons onion, minced
1 cup milk
1 pound crab meat, cartilage removed

Pre-heat oven to 350°F.
Mix together cream cheese, onion, and milk. Fold in crabmeat. Place mixture in greased casserole. Bake, covered, for 30 minutes. Serve hot with crackers.

Tuna-Cheese Spread

APPROXIMATELY 1¼ CUPS

1 7-ounce can tuna, drained and flaked
1/2 cup cheddar cheese, shredded
1/2 cup mayonnaise
1 tablespoon onion, grated
1 teaspoon prepared horseradish
French bread, toast squares, or crackers

Pre-heat broiler.
Combine all ingredients. Spread on toast squares, rounds of toasted French bread, or crackers. Broil until bubbly and browned. Serve immediately. This can also be served cold as a dip.

Cream of Asparagus Soup

6 SERVINGS

1 pound fresh asparagus spears, chopped
1 medium onion, chopped
2 cups chicken broth
2 tablespoons butter or margarine
2 tablespoons flour
1 cup light cream
1/8 teaspoon pepper
Salt, to taste

Combine chopped asparagus, onion, and chicken broth in saucepan. Simmer until vegetables are tender. Puree cooled mixture in blender or food processor until smooth.
Melt butter in saucepan and blend in flour, stirring constantly 1 to 2 minutes.
Gradually add puree, stirring constantly. Slowly add cream, salt, and pepper. Heat slowly, but do not boil.

Pea Pod Soup

Peanut Soup

4 SERVINGS

½ cup celery, diced
1 small onion, minced
4 tablespoons butter
1½ tablespoons flour
1¾ cups chicken broth
½ cup creamy peanut butter
½ cup light cream
Parsley, to garnish
Peanuts, to garnish

Sauté celery and onion in melted butter until onion is transparent. Stir in flour and mix until smooth.
Gradually add chicken broth, stirring constantly. Bring to a boil, add peanut butter and simmer for 20 minutes, stirring frequently.
To serve, stir in cream and heat. Garnish with parsley and peanuts.

Pea Pod Soup

4 SERVINGS

2 pounds pea pods
1 onion, peeled and sliced
2 to 3 sprigs fresh mint
2 to 3 sprigs parsley
4 cups stock or 2 bouillon cubes and 4 cups water
Salt, pepper and sugar, to taste
4 tablespoons cooked green peas
Chopped fresh mint, to garnish

Wash pea pods and put into large stockpot with onion, mint, parsley, and stock. Bring to a boil, cover, and simmer for approximately 40 minutes.
When outer flesh of the pods is tender, rub through a sieve or food mill. Add salt, pepper, and sugar to taste.
Add whole, cooked peas and sprinkle with chopped mint before serving.

Beef Tartare

Beef Tartare

4 SERVINGS

1 pound chuck, round sirloin, or tenderloin steak
Freshly ground black pepper, to taste
4 large rings raw onion
4 raw egg yolks
2 teaspoons capers
4 anchovy fillets
4 quarters lemon

Buy and grind the steak as close to serving time as possible. Season only with pepper.

Shape the meat into 4 equal sized cakes; make a depression in the center of each with a spoon. Place an onion ring around the depression and put an egg yolk into the center. Sprinkle several capers on top of the egg yolk and lay one curled anchovy fillet on top of each yolk. Garnish with chives or fresh horseradish if desired.

Serve with rye bread and butter, or French bread and lemon quarters.

Clam Dip

8 SERVINGS

2 6-ounce cans clams, minced
2 tablespoons butter
2 cloves garlic, minced
1 small onion, minced
¼ teaspoon oregano
½ teaspoon parsley
4 strips bacon, cooked and crumbled
¼ cup Italian-style bread crumbs
Parmesan cheese, grated, to garnish

Pre-heat oven to 350°F.

Drain 1 can clams and discard liquid. Reserve liquid from other can.

Sauté onion and garlic in butter. Add oregano, parsley, crumbs, clams, liquid, and 2 strips of crumbled bacon. Mix well.

Put into greased 1-quart casserole. Sprinkle with remaining strips of crumbled bacon and Parmesan cheese. Bake for 25 minutes.

Pizza Rolls

5 DOZEN ROLLS

1½ 8-ounce cans tomato sauce
1½ cups vegetable oil
4 green onions, finely chopped
¾ green pepper, finely chopped
1 pound sharp cheese, grated
5 dozen small rolls with soft insides removed

Pre-heat oven to 350°F.

Mix together tomato sauce, oil, onions, pepper, and cheese. Fill center of rolls. Bake for 20 minutes.

Orange Soup

6 SERVINGS

1 tablespoon cornstarch
4 cups water
1½ cups orange juice
¼ cup sugar
Whipped cream, to garnish
Orange slices, to garnish

Mix cornstarch in ¼ cup cold water. Bring remaining water to a boil. Add cornstarch mixture to boiling water, stirring constantly until slightly thickened. Add orange juice and sugar. Serve hot or cold, garnished with spoonful of whipped cream and thin orange slice.

Beef Vegetable Soup

2 SERVINGS

½ pound ground beef
½ cup onion, chopped
2 cups hot water
¾ cup celery, chopped
¾ cup potatoes, chopped
1 teaspoon salt
¼ teaspoon pepper
½ bay leaf, crumbled
Pinch of basil
3 whole tomatoes, stems removed

Brown ground beef in heavy soup pot. Add onion and sauté for 5 minutes. Add remaining ingredients, except tomatoes. Mix thoroughly, scraping browned beef crust from bottom of pot.

Bring to a boil, cover, simmer for 20 minutes. Add tomatoes and more water, if necessary. Simmer for 10 minutes.

Spanokopita

8 SERVINGS

Filling:
2 pounds fresh spinach
1 cup onion, chopped
2 tablespoons butter
2 cups feta cheese, crumbled
3 tablespoons butter
2 tablespoons flour
2 cups cottage cheese
5 eggs
1 teaspoon basil
½ teaspoon oregano
Salt and pepper, to taste
Dough:
1 package phyllo dough, defrosted
1 cup butter, melted
1 tablespoon anise or fennel seeds

Pre-heat oven to 375°F.

Clean, stem, and chop spinach. Salt lightly and simmer, adding no water, for 5 minutes. Sauté onions in butter, until transparent, salting lightly. Combine with spinach and remaining filling ingredients.

Pour ¾ cup melted butter in 9 x 5-inch baking pan. Place layer of phyllo dough in pan with edges lining sides of pan. Brush generously with butter.

Continue layering dough, brushing each layer with butter. When 8 layers have been placed in pan, spread on half of filling. Continue with another 8 layers of dough and butter, then apply remaining filling, spreading it to edges.

Fold excess phyllo dough down along edges, making neat corners. Continue with layers of phyllo and butter until pan is filled. Butter top layer and sprinkle with tablespoon of anise or fennel seeds.

Bake 45 minutes, or until golden brown.

Rumaki

8 SERVINGS

1 8-ounce can water chestnuts, drained and halved
½ cup soy sauce
Brown sugar, to sprinkle
Soy sauce, to taste
Bacon strips, to garnish

Pre-heat broiler.

Soak chestnuts in soy sauce for 4 hours or overnight. Cut bacon strips in half. Roll bacon around chestnut and secure with toothpick. Sprinkle heavily with brown sugar. Broil until bacon is crisp.

VEGETABLES & SALADS

Sweet Potato Puffs

4 SERVINGS

2 cups sweet potatoes, cooked
Salt and pepper, to taste
2 tablespoons brown sugar
1 egg, beaten
Bread crumbs, to dredge
Oil, to deep-fry

Mash together potatoes, seasonings, sugar, and egg. Form into balls and roll in bread crumbs. Drop into 375-400°F oil and fry until golden brown. Drain well.

Bean Sprout Salad

6 SERVINGS

1 pound fresh bean sprouts
1/2 pound fresh mushrooms, sliced
1/2 cup vegetable oil
2 tablespoons vinegar
Juice of 1 lemon
2 tablespoons soy sauce
1 teaspoon prepared mustard
1/2 teaspoon paprika
2 tablespoons pimento, chopped
1 teaspoon salt
1/2 teaspoon pepper
1/2 green pepper, chopped, to garnish

Rinse sprouts under cold water; drain well. Rinse mushrooms and dry.
Combine oil, vinegar, lemon juice, soy sauce, mustard, paprika, pimento, salt, and pepper in jar with lid. Shake well.
Before serving, pour dressing over vegetables and mix well. Garnish with green pepper.

Stuffed Eggplant

4 SERVINGS

2 firm medium eggplants
Boiling salted water
1/2 cup olive oil
2 garlic cloves, peeled and minced
1 small onion, peeled and chopped
3 cups mushrooms, thickly sliced
1 1/2 teaspoons oregano, crumbled
1 teaspoon sweet basil, crumbled
1 teaspoon salt
2 small green peppers, chopped
2 small fresh tomatoes, cut in wedges
1 12-ounce can artichoke hearts, drained and halved
1 cup Parmesan cheese, grated

Pre-heat oven to 350°F.
Halve eggplants lengthwise. Peel 1/2 inch skin around edge of each half. Scoop pulp from center to form shells, being careful not to pierce eggplant skin. Dice pulp. Parboil shells in 1-inch boiling salted water until barely tender. Drain well and set aside.
Heat oil in heavy skillet. Sauté garlic, onion, and mushrooms until mushroom liquid evaporates. Add eggplant pulp; sauté until lightly browned. Add seasonings. Gently stir in peppers, tomatoes, and artichoke hearts. Heat thoroughly. Stir in 1/2 cup Parmesan cheese.
Place reserved eggplant shells cut side up in lightly greased baking dish. Mound vegetable mixture in shells. Sprinkle with remaining cheese. Bake for 20 minutes.

Cranberry Salad

6 SERVINGS

1 envelope unflavored gelatin
1/4 cup cold water
1/2 cup hot water
1 7-ounce can cranberry sauce
1/4 teaspoon salt
1/2 cup celery, chopped
1/2 cup nuts, chopped

Soften gelatin in cold water, then dissolve in hot water. Pour over cranberry sauce. Beat with rotary beater until softened to smooth mixture. When mixture begins to thicken, add celery and nuts.
Pour into greased 2-cup mold. Chill, but do not freeze.

Beef and Macaroni Casserole

Beef and Macaroni Casserole

6 SERVINGS

3 tablespoons cooking fat
2 cups finely chopped onion
2 garlic cloves, crushed
1/2 cup sliced mushrooms
1 pound ground beef
1 30-ounce can peeled tomatoes
1 tablespoon chopped parsley
1 8-ounce package macaroni
1 to 2 tablespoons margarine
Grated Parmesan or sharp cheddar cheese, to garnish

Heat fat in saucepan. Add onion, garlic, and mushrooms, and sauté until onion becomes pale yellow in color. Add meat and stir until browned.

Add tomatoes, parsley, and season to taste. Cover and simmer for approximately 45 minutes.

While meat is cooking, prepare macaroni according to package instructions. Drain well and toss with margarine. Place macaroni on hot platter, pour meat sauce over, and sprinkle with grated cheese.

Turkey Salad

8 SERVINGS

2 cups turkey, chopped
1/4 cup celery, thinly sliced in crescents
2 tablespoons pimento, finely chopped
2 tablespoons capers
1 tablespoon green onion, finely chopped
1 tablespoon parsley, finely chopped
1/2 cup mayonnaise
1 teaspoon Dijon-style mustard
Salt, to taste
Tabasco sauce, to taste
1/2 lemon
Bibb lettuce, to garnish

Combine turkey, celery, pimento, capers, green onion and parsley. Toss ingredients together. Mix mayonnaise and mustard, season to taste. Toss salad with mayonnaise and mustard.

To serve, arrange on Bibb lettuce leaves and squeeze lemon over salad.

Ratatouille Salad

4 SERVINGS

2 eggplants
Coarse salt, to sprinkle
1/2 cup olive oil
1 onion, peeled and chopped
1 large red pepper, seeded and cut into small pieces
4 tomatoes, peeled and chopped
2 garlic cloves, crushed
12 coriander seeds
Chopped basil or parsley, to garnish

Wipe eggplants, cut into 1/2-inch squares, and put into colander. Sprinkle with coarse salt and drain for 20 minutes. Rinse with cool water.

Heat 2 tablespoons of the oil in a skillet and sauté the onion for approximately 10 minutes or until it begins to soften. Add an additional tablespoon of oil, put in rinsed eggplant and red pepper, and simmer for 30 to 40 minutes.

Add tomatoes, garlic, and coriander, and continue to cook until tomatoes are soft, adding remainder of oil if necessary. Season to taste, then chill.

Before serving, drain off excess oil and sprinkle with basil or parsley.

Carrots in White Wine

6 SERVINGS

2 pounds carrots, scraped and cut into 1/4 inch slices
1 1/2 cups celery, diced
1/2 cup onion, chopped
3/4 cup white wine
1/4 cup sugar
1/4 cup butter
1 teaspoon dill
Salt and pepper, to taste

Mix together all ingredients in a large saucepan. Cook, covered, over low heat, until carrots are just tender.

Ratatouille Salad

Stuffed Peppers

6 SERVINGS

6 large green peppers
3 tablespoons olive oil
1 small onion, finely chopped
1 large carrot, shredded
1/2 teaspoon basil
1/2 teaspoon oregano
2 garlic cloves, crushed
1 cup rice, cooked
Salt and pepper, to taste
1 1/2 cups mozzarella cheese, grated
2 eggs, beaten
1 cup tomato juice

Pre-heat oven to 350°F.

Cut tops off peppers; remove stems and seeds. Steam until slightly tender, approximately 8 to 10 minutes. Cool.

Heat oil and sauté onion and carrot until tender. Add herbs and garlic as onions begin to soften. Remove from heat and mix with cooked rice. Salt and pepper to taste. Stir in cheese and eggs. Spoon into prepared peppers and set upright in shallow baking dish. Pour tomato juice over peppers, cover, and bake for 20 to 25 minutes or until stuffing is set.

Baked Tomatoes

6 SERVINGS

24 plum tomatoes
5 tablespoons butter
1 bay leaf
Juice of one small garlic clove
1 9-ounce package frozen chopped spinach
1 1/2 teaspoons lemon juice
1/4 teaspoon nutmeg
2 drops of Tabasco sauce
Salt, to taste
2 tablespoons Parmesan cheese, grated

Pre-heat oven to 350°F.

Cut slice off bottom of tomatoes. Scoop out pulp and juice. Turn upside down to drain.

Melt 3 tablespoons of butter in medium skillet. Add bay leaf and garlic juice. Simmer for two to three minutes. Discard bay leaf. Stir in spinach, lemon juice, nutmeg, Tabasco, and salt. Remove from heat.

Place tomatoes in baking dish. Sprinkle cavities with salt. Stuff with spinach mixture. Sprinkle tops with cheese. Melt remaining butter. Spoon over cheese. Bake for 20 minutes.

Date and Cabbage Salad

6 SERVINGS

2 cups red cabbage, shredded
2 cups green cabbage, shredded
1 cup dates, diced
3 tablespoons lemon or lime juice
2 tablespoons honey
1/2 cup vegetable oil
1/8 teaspoon salt

Mix cabbages and dates in salad bowl. Blend remaining ingredients in blender or shake well in a jar. Chill in refrigerator. Shake dressing again before tossing with cabbages and dates.

Chinese Noodle Salad

8 SERVINGS

4 cups fine egg noodles, uncooked
1/4 cup soy sauce
2 teaspoons vegetable oil
1 teaspoon white vinegar
1/2 teaspoon sugar
1/4 teaspoon garlic powder
1/4 teaspoon ginger
1 cup radishes, thinly sliced
1 rib celery, cleaned and thinly sliced in crescents
1 tablespoon sesame seeds, toasted

Cook noodles according to package directions, under-cooking slightly. Rinse with cold water, drain well, and set aside. In large bowl, combine soy sauce, oil, vinegar, sugar, garlic, and ginger. Add radishes, celery, and noodles. Toss lightly until mixed. Sprinkle with sesame seeds.

Sauerkraut Salad

6 SERVINGS

1 16-ounce can sauerkraut, drained
1 cup celery, diced
1/2 cup green pepper, diced
1/2 cup onion, diced
1 3-ounce can pimento, chopped
1 teaspoon salt
1 1/2 cups sugar
1/4 cup vinegar
1/4 cup vegetable oil

Combine all ingredients and chill for several hours. Salad keeps well when refrigerated.

FISH & SEAFOOD

Baked Scallops

4 SERVINGS

1 pound bay scallops
Salt and pepper, to taste
1 egg
2 tablespoons water
¾ cup fine bread crumbs
¼ cup butter, melted
Parsley, to garnish

Pre-heat oven to 450°F.

Wipe scallops dry. Season with salt and pepper. Beat together egg and water. Dip scallops first in egg, then in crumbs, then in melted butter. Place in shallow baking dish. Bake for 20 to 25 minutes. Garnish with parsley.

Lobster Thermidor

6 SERVINGS

6 tablespoons butter or margarine
4 tablespoons flour
5 tablespoons sherry
Pinch of nutmeg
Pinch of paprika
Pinch of salt
1 cup light cream
3 packages langostino lobster
½ cup cheddar cheese, grated

Pre-heat oven to 350°F.

Melt butter in double boiler. Stir in flour, sherry, nutmeg, paprika, and salt. Slowly add cream, stirring constantly.

Squeeze excess liquid from langostino and stir into sauce. Pour into casserole and bake for 30 minutes. Sprinkle cheese on top and return to oven for 10 minutes or until cheese is bubbly.

Poached Red Snapper

6 SERVINGS

1 whole red snapper, about 3½ pounds, cleaned and
   scaled
Salt and pepper, to taste
⅓ cup butter or margarine, melted
1 teaspoon lemon rind, grated
¼ cup parsley, chopped
1 4-ounce jar pimiento, drained and diced
1 red onion, thinly sliced
½ cup chicken broth
Lemon slices, to garnish

Pre-heat oven to 350°F.

Sprinkle red snapper inside and out with salt and pepper. Combine butter and lemon rind, and brush fish on all sides. Place on square of heavy-duty aluminum foil. Drizzle remaining butter mixture over snapper. Sprinkle with remaining ingredients. Seal foil tightly. Bake for 35 to 40 minutes.

Carefully remove foil from fish and reserve cooking juices. Place fish on serving platter and pour cooking juices over fish. Garnish with lemon slices.

Creamed Oysters and Shrimp

4 SERVINGS

1 pint fresh oysters, shucked
½ pound shrimp, cooked
¼ cup sherry
¼ cup butter
1½ tablespoons flour
½ teaspoon salt
Dash of cayenne pepper
Dash of nutmeg
1 cup light cream
2 egg yolks, lightly beaten
2 tablespoons brandy
Toast points, English muffins, or patty shells

Simmer oysters approximately 7 minutes. Drain well. Shell cooked shrimp, devein and cut into pieces. Add to oysters, pour sherry over mixture and marinate at least 1 hour.

Add butter and simmer for 5 minutes. Combine flour and seasonings and stir into mixture. Simmer 2 to 3 minutes. Add cream and stir until mixture thickens. Stir in egg yolks and brandy.

Serve on toast points, toasted English muffins, or in patty shells.

Shrimp and Rice Casserole

Shrimp and Rice Casserole

4 SERVINGS

4 slices bacon
1 small onion, peeled and chopped
1 cup rice
1 30-ounce can tomatoes
1 cup water
1 bay leaf
½ pound fresh shrimp or scampi, peeled and deveined

Pre-heat oven to 350°F.

Dice bacon and brown until crisp. Remove from pan and drain on paper towel.

Add onion and rice to bacon fat and stir over low heat for approximately 5 minutes. Transfer to a stove-top casserole. Add tomatoes, water, seasoning, and bay leaf. Cover and cook for 30 minutes.

Add bacon and shrimp and cook for another 10 minutes.

Scalloped Oysters

6 SERVINGS

1 quart oysters, drained
2 tablespoons parsley, minced
2 tablespoons shallots, minced
¼ teaspoon salt
¼ teaspoon pepper
1 teaspoon lemon juice
½ cup cracker crumbs
⅓ cup butter
¾ cup milk

Pre-heat oven to 350°F.

Butter shallow 1-quart casserole and place a layer of oysters on bottom. Sprinkle with parsley, shallots, salt, pepper, lemon juice, and crumbs. Dot with butter. Repeat another layer. Pour milk over casserole and bake for 30 minutes.

Seafood Pie

Seafood Pie

8 SERVINGS

Pastry for a 9-inch one-crust pie
3 tablespoons butter or margarine
3 tablespoons finely chopped green onions
1½ cups diced, cooked seafood
1 tablespoon tomato paste
Cayenne pepper, to taste
3 tablespoons sherry
4 eggs
1½ cups heavy cream
¼ cup grated Gruyère cheese

Pre-heat oven to 375°F.

Line a 9-inch pie plate with the pastry, prick the bottom, and bake for 15 minutes. Remove from heat and let cool.

Melt butter in skillet, add onion, and sauté for approximately 2 minutes. Add seafood and stir over low heat for 2 minutes. Add tomato paste, cayenne pepper, and sherry. Stir until boiling. Remove from heat and allow to cool.

Beat eggs, add cream, and stir in cooled seafood mixture. Season to taste and pour into pastry shell. Sprinkle with cheese and bake for 25 to 30 minutes at 350°F

Serve in wedge-shaped slices.

Baked Oysters

6 SERVINGS

2 tablespoons butter or margarine
1 cup fresh white bread crumbs
1 teaspoon garlic, minced
2 tablespoons parsley, finely chopped
2 dozen freshly shucked oysters, drained
3 tablespoons Parmesan cheese, grated

Pre-heat oven to 450°F.
Grease an 8 x 10-inch ovenproof dish.
In skillet, melt butter or margarine over moderate heat. Sauté bread crumbs and garlic, 2 to 3 minutes or until crisp and golden. Stir in parsley.
Spread ⅔ cup of sautéed mixture in bottom of baking dish. Arrange oysters over it in 1 layer. Mix remaining bread crumb mixture with grated cheese and spread over oysters. Dot with butter or margarine.
Bake in top third of oven for 12 to 15 minutes or until juices bubble. This dish can be prepared in advance and refrigerated before baking.

Shrimp Bake

4 SERVINGS

1 pound frozen shrimp, shelled and deveined
1 8-ounce package cream cheese
¼ cup butter, softened
1 tablespoon flour
1 tablespoon sugar
¼ teaspoon dry mustard
¼ teaspoon fresh basil
Salt, to taste
2 tablespoons fresh lemon juice
Topping:
½ cup fine dry bread crumbs
¼ cup butter, melted

Pre-heat oven to 375°F.
Cook shrimp according to package directions. Divide shrimp into 4 ramekins.
Heat cream cheese over low heat or in top of a double boiler until softened. Stir in softened butter until mixture is creamed. Remove from heat.
Combine flour, sugar, mustard, basil and salt, blend into cream cheese mixture. Stir in lemon juice. Simmer over low heat, stirring constantly until thickened. Pour over shrimp.
Mix crumbs and butter and sprinkle over sauce. Bake 12 minutes. Serve immediately.

Fish Fillets Parmesan

6 SERVINGS

2 pounds fish fillets
1 cup sour cream
¼ cup Parmesan cheese, grated
1 tablespoon lemon juice
1 tablespoon onion, grated
½ teaspoon salt
⅛ teaspoon Tabasco sauce
Dash of paprika
Parsley, chopped, to garnish

Pre-heat oven to 350°F.
Cut fillets into serving-size portions. Place in well-greased baking dish.
Combine sour cream, Parmesan cheese, lemon juice, onion, salt, and Tabasco sauce. Spread mixture over fish and sprinkle with paprika. Bake for 25 to 30 minutes or until fish flakes easily with a fork.
Garnish with chopped parsley.

Fish Steaks with Pears

4 SERVINGS

2 tablespoons butter
1 cup onion, thinly sliced
1 cup carrots, julienned
2 Bartlett pears, fresh and firm
½ teaspoon salt
½ teaspoon dry mustard
¼ teaspoon fresh basil, crumbled
¼ teaspoon fresh dill, crumbled
1 ½ pounds firm fish fillets, sea bass, haddock or salmon
2 small tomatoes, sliced
1 lemon, thinly sliced

Melt 1 tablespoon butter in large skillet. Add onion and carrot and stir to mix well. Cover skillet and simmer 5 to 10 minutes.
Pare, quarter and core pears. Melt remaining butter. Mix with salt, mustard, basil and dill. Toss with pears.
Add fish fillets to pears and butter mixture. Stir in tomatoes and lemon slices.
Cover and simmer 10 minutes, or until fish almost flakes easily with a fork.

MEATS

Lamb with Cabbage

6 SERVINGS

1 tablespoon butter
1 tablespoon flour
¼ cup water
2 pounds lamb
1 head cabbage
1 teaspoon salt
¼ teaspoon ground pepper
Water, to cover

Melt butter in 3-quart pot. Mix flour with water and add to melted butter, stirring to a paste consistency. Remove from heat.

Cut lamb into bite-size pieces. Wash and drain cabbage and cut into small pieces. Put a layer of cabbage on top of paste in pot. Add a layer of lamb. Season each layer with salt and pepper and continue layering the cabbage and meat, ending with cabbage.

Pour in just enough water to cover meat and cabbage. Bring to a boil, then simmer until meat is tender, at least 1 hour. Do not stir.

Serve in layers.

Three-Meat Stew

4 SERVINGS

1½ pounds stew beef, diced
½ pound fresh pork, diced
2 cups beef stock
1½ cups cooked corned beef, diced
4 cups raw potatoes, cut in small pieces
1 onion, diced
1 teaspoon salt
½ teaspoon freshly ground pepper

Simmer raw beef and pork for 30 minutes with enough stock to cover. Add remainder of ingredients and simmer for at least 1 hour or until meat is tender.

Orange-Ginger Pork Roast

12 SERVINGS

1 3- to 4-pound boneless pork loin roast
1 teaspoon dry mustard
1 teaspoon salt
½ teaspoon white pepper
½ teaspoon ground ginger
Glaze:
1 cup orange marmalade
¼ cup light corn syrup
2 tablespoons lemon juice
½ teaspoon dry mustard
½ teaspoon ground ginger

Pre-heat oven to 325°F.

Combine dry mustard, salt, white pepper, and ginger. Mix well and rub into roast. Set aside.

To make glaze, combine all ingredients and simmer over medium heat for 5 minutes, stirring frequently.

Place roast on rack in shallow pan. Insert meat thermometer with bulb in the center of the thickest part of roast. Bake, uncovered, for 35 to 40 minutes per pound or until thermometer registers 170 degrees. Baste with glaze every 10 minutes during last 30 minutes of cooking time.

Let roast stand 10 minutes before carving to allow juices to set.

Beef Rolls

6 SERVINGS

3 pounds top round steak, 1½ inches thick
1 pound ground veal
1 cup onions, chopped
½ cup bread crumbs
1 egg
1 cup chili sauce
Flour seasoned with salt and pepper, to taste

Pre-heat oven to 450°F.

Pound steak to ½-inch thickness. In mixing bowl, combine veal, onions, bread crumbs, egg, and chili sauce. Spread filling over round steak slices and roll up the meat. Tie each roll with a string. Cover outside of rolls with seasoned flour.

Brown rolls for 10 to 15 minutes; reduce heat to 350°F, and roast for 1½ hours.

Slice and serve. Beef rolls can also be prepared in advance and served cold.

Preparing for Market

Hunter's Turkey

6 SERVINGS

Hunter's sauce:
3 tablespoons vegetable oil
1 onion, chopped
1 garlic clove, crushed
2 tablespoons flour
4 tablespoons tomato puree
¼ cup white wine
1 cup brown stock
8 mushrooms, sliced
2 tablespoons butter
1 tablespoon chopped parsley
½ teaspoon oregano
Casserole:
8 slices turkey
4 tablespoons grated cheese
2 tablespoons bread crumbs

Pre-heat oven to 350°F. To make Hunter's sauce, heat vegetable oil in skillet. Sauté chopped onion and crushed garlic until golden brown. Sprinkle in flour and sauté for 5 minutes, stirring constantly.

Add tomato puree, wine and stock. Bring to a boil, stirring frequently. Sauté sliced mushrooms in butter for 3 minutes. Add to skillet. Stir in parsley and oregano and simmer for 3 minutes.

For the casserole, place turkey slices in bottom of ovenproof casserole. Pour the sauce over the turkey slices. Bake for 15 minutes. Pre-heat broiler. Remove casserole from oven and sprinkle with cheese and bread crumbs. Place under broiler until cheese melts and bread crumbs brown. Serve hot.

The Farmer's Home—Harvest

Veal Stew

8 SERVINGS

4 pounds veal cubes
3 tablespoons vegetable oil
4 tablespoons flour
1 teaspoon thyme
1 tablespoon salt
Dash of pepper
4 onions, minced
2 cups dry white wine
2 cups chicken broth
6 ripe tomatoes, chopped
2 cloves garlic
1 large strip orange or lemon rind
1 bay leaf
4 sprigs parsley
1 pound mushrooms, sliced

Pre-heat oven to 325°F.
Sauté veal cubes in a heavy skillet in 2 tablespoons vegetable oil until brown. Remove to 4 to 5-quart stove-top casserole. Mix flour with thyme, salt and pepper. Sprinkle mixture over veal and toss until veal is well-coated.
Brown onions in remaining oil. Add white wine and boil for 1 minute, stirring occasionally. Pour onion-wine mixture over veal. Add chicken broth and tomatoes to casserole. Stir in garlic, orange or lemon rind, bay leaf, and parsley.
Bring stew to a boil on top of stove. Remove to oven and bake for 1 hour to 1 hour and 15 minutes or until veal is almost tender. Add mushrooms, basting with sauce. Continue cooking for 15 minutes.

Pork Chops with Prunes

8 SERVINGS

30 pitted prunes
1 cup dry red wine
8 pork chops, about 1/4 pound each
Salt and pepper, to taste
2 tablespoons vegetable oil
1/2 cup onion, finely chopped
3/4 cup chicken broth
2 tablespoons butter

Place prunes in saucepan and cover with wine. Bring to a boil and simmer for 15 minutes or until almost all wine is evaporated.
Sprinkle chops on both sides with salt and pepper. Heat oil in heavy skillet and add chops. Sauté until browned on one side, approximately 5 minutes. Turn and brown on other side for 5 minutes. Continue cooking, turning chops occasionally, for 5 minutes. Transfer to warm serving dish.
Pour off almost all fat from skillet. Sauté onion in skillet, stirring until lightly browned. Add broth and stir to dissolve particles that cling to bottom of pan. Add prunes and any liquid that remains in saucepan. Swirl butter into sauce and pour over chops.

Roast Brisket of Beef

8 SERVINGS

5 pounds beef brisket
2 teaspoons salt
1/4 teaspoon pepper
2 onions, sliced
4 celery ribs
1 cup chili sauce
1/4 cup water
1 can beer

Pre-heat oven to 325°F.
Place beef in roasting pan, fat side up. Season with salt and pepper. Place onions, celery, and chili sauce over beef. Add water around sides of pan.
Roast uncovered, basting often with pan drippings, until meat is well-browned. Then cover.
After 3½ hours, pour beer over roast. Cover and cook for additional 1½ hours or until tender. Remove meat and cool. Strain gravy and cool. Skim off as much fat as possible. Slice meat and reheat in skimmed gravy. Add water if necessary.

Rack of Lamb

4 SERVINGS

4 tablespoons margarine, melted
1 tablespoon shallots, chopped
1 teaspoon garlic, chopped
1/4 cup parsley, chopped
1/2 cup fresh bread crumbs
1 well-trimmed rack of lamb, about 1½ to 1¾ pounds, with backbone removed
Salt and pepper, to taste

Pre-heat oven to 425°F.
Mix together margarine, shallots, garlic, parsley, and crumbs. Set aside.
Season lamb with salt and pepper and brown in an ovenproof skillet over high heat for 5 to 6 minutes. Cover meat with crumb mixture. Roast in oven for 10 to 14 minutes per pound. Let lamb rest 5 to 10 minutes before serving.
To serve, carve as individual chops or in slices. Serve on heated plates.

POULTRY

Ducklings in Wine

8 SERVINGS

2 ducklings, 4 to 5 pounds each, cut into serving pieces
2 cups red wine
½ cup brandy
2 onions, chopped
1 garlic clove, slivered
8 parsley sprigs, minced
1 bay leaf
Pinch of ground thyme
¼ cup vegetable oil
2 cups mushrooms, sliced
Salt and pepper, to taste

Wash ducklings and dry. Combine wine, brandy, onions, garlic, parsley, bay leaf, and thyme and pour over duckling pieces. Marinate for 5 hours, turning pieces occasionally. Drain pieces and set aside. Press marinade through fine sieve or whirl in blender.

Heat vegetable oil in a heavy skillet. Brown duckling pieces in hot oil. Remove from skillet and place in a heavy kettle and add marinade. Bring to a boil, cover and simmer for 1½ to 2 hours, or until pieces are tender. Add mushrooms and cook for 15 minutes longer. Spoon off fat and season to taste.

Roast Cornish Hens

4 SERVINGS

2 Cornish hens, skinned and cut in half
1 garlic clove, sliced in half
Salt and pepper, to taste
½ cup butter or margarine
1 tablespoon tarragon
1 teaspoon parsley, minced

Pre-heat oven to 350°F.

Rub hens with garlic. Salt and pepper lightly. Place in lightly greased baking dish. Melt butter; add tarragon and parsley, mixing well. Baste hens with mixture. Roast for 1 hour, basting every 15 minutes.

Chicken Pot Pie

6 SERVINGS

3½ cups all-purpose flour
½ teaspoon baking powder
Pinch of salt
4 tablespoons water
8 cups chicken broth
2½ to 3 cups chicken meat, cooked
3 medium potatoes, peeled and chopped
Parsley, to garnish

Mix together flour, baking powder, and salt. Add just enough water to make a soft dough that can be rolled. Roll as thin as possible and cut into 1 x 2-inch squares.

In large pot, bring broth and chicken to a boil. Add potatoes and simmer until potatoes can just be pierced with a fork.

Add dough squares, several at a time, stirring slightly so dough does not stick together. When all squares have been added, reduce heat and simmer until dough squares are tender.

Garnish with chopped parsley.

English Country Chicken

4 SERVINGS

2½ to 3 pound chicken, cut into pieces and skinned
1 16-ounce jar orange marmalade
⅓ cup prepared mustard
1 teaspoon curry powder
½ teaspoon salt
2 tablespoons lemon juice
½ cup water
2 tablespoons cornstarch

Pre-heat oven to 375°F.

Arrange chicken in 2-quart shallow baking dish. Heat marmalade, mustard, curry powder, and salt in a saucepan until marmalade melts. Stir in lemon juice, and pour mixture over chicken.

Cover baking dish with foil. Bake for 45 minutes. Remove foil and baste. Bake uncovered for 30 minutes longer. Remove chicken to serving platter.

Pour remaining mixture into a saucepan. Combine water and cornstarch and blend into mixture. Simmer, stirring constantly, until thickened.

To serve, pour sauce over chicken.

French Roast Chicken

French Roast Chicken

6 SERVINGS

Chicken giblets
1 onion
1½ cups water
1 chicken, 3 to 4 pounds
6 to 7 tablespoons butter
3 to 4 sprigs fresh parsley
2 to 3 slices bacon
1 bunch watercress, to garnish

Pre-heat oven to 350°F.

Combine giblets, onion and water, season to taste and simmer for 15 minutes.

Put half the butter inside bird with parsley. Spread remaining butter over chicken, and cover with bacon slices. Place in roasting pan, and pour half the stock over chicken. Roast in oven, basting with stock every 15 minutes and turning chicken from side to side. Allow 20 minutes per pound.

During last 20 minutes, remove bacon slices and place bird breast side up to brown.

Place chicken on a hot platter and keep warm in oven. Skim butter from top of pan drippings. Add remaining stock to roasting pan and boil until well-flavored. Serve as gravy.

Serve chicken either hot or cold with a green salad and garnished with watercress.

Chicken in Red Wine

2 SERVINGS

2 fryer thighs
½ medium onion, thinly sliced
½ cup mushrooms, sliced
1 16-ounce can tomatoes, undrained
1 garlic clove, minced
¼ teaspoon dried rosemary
Pinch of dried thyme
Pinch of dried savory
Pinch of dried basil
¼ cup Canadian-style bacon, diced
7 tablespoons dry red wine
1 tablespoon flour

Pre-heat broiler.

Broil chicken thighs skin-side up until skin is crisp.

Set oven temperature to 350°F. Grease 1-quart oven-proof casserole. Arrange onion and mushrooms in bottom of casserole. Mash tomatoes with garlic and herbs, and spoon into casserole. Add diced bacon. Arrange browned chicken thighs on top, skin-side up. Pour over 4 tablespoons wine. Cover casserole and bake 45 to 50 minutes. Uncover casserole and bake additional 10 to 15 minutes.

Blend flour with remaining 3 tablespoons wine. Stir into tomato mixture, without removing chicken. Bake an additional 5 to 10 minutes, uncovered, until sauce thickens.

Chicken Cacciatore

6 SERVINGS

3½ pound chicken, cut in pieces
3 tablespoons olive oil
4 tablespoons unsalted butter
1 large onion, minced
3 cloves garlic, minced
½ cup parsley, minced
3 chicken livers, diced
6 large mushrooms, diced
1 teaspoon rosemary
2 large tomatoes, peeled, cored, and chopped
Freshly ground pepper, to taste
Cooked pasta tossed with olive oil

Pre-heat oven to 350°F.

Wipe chicken pieces with damp cloth. Heat oil in heavy-bottomed frying pan and sauté chicken until golden brown. Transfer chicken to a 3-quart baking dish.

Add butter to pan drippings and sauté onion, garlic, and parsley for 4 to 5 minutes. Add chicken livers, mushrooms, and rosemary. Sauté until vegetables are limp. Stir in tomatoes and cook, covered, for 5 minutes.

Spoon vegetable mixture over chicken and sprinkle with pepper. Bake, covered, for 35 to 40 minutes or until chicken is tender. Serve over pasta.

Home to Thanksgiving

Sunday Supper

4 SERVINGS

1 chicken, cut up
¼ cup butter, melted
Salt and pepper, to taste
½ cup apricot preserves
⅓ cup orange juice
¼ to ½ teaspoon ginger
Dash allspice
4 medium sweet potatoes, cooked, peeled and halved

Place chicken, skin side down, on foil-covered boiler rack. Brush with 1 tablespoon butter and sprinkle with salt and pepper. Broil 6 to 7 inches from heat source for 20 minutes or until chicken is golden brown on one side. Turn chicken and broil 10 to 15 minutes longer.

Combine preserves, orange juice, spices and salt with remaining melted butter in a small saucepan.

Place sweet potatoes on broiler rack with chicken. Brush chicken and potatoes with apricot preserves mixture and broil 1 minute. Turn sweet potatoes and chicken, brush with apricot mixture and broil 1 minute longer.

Serve remaining apricot preserves sauce with the sweet potatoes and chicken.

White Chicken Cacciatore

2 SERVINGS

2 tablespoons olive oil
2 chicken breast halves
Salt and pepper, to taste
1 small yellow onion, sliced
6 fresh mushrooms, washed and sliced
1 garlic clove, crushed
⅓ cup dry white wine or apple juice

Heat oil in a 10-inch skillet over high heat until almost smoking. Sprinkle chicken with salt and pepper. Brown chicken, 6 to 8 minutes, turning twice.

Push chicken to side of pan, add onion and mushrooms and sauté until onion is transparent. Add garlic and sauté 1 minute. Add wine or apple juice, bring mixture to a simmer and reduce heat.

Cover skillet and simmer for 20 minutes or until chicken is tender. Turn chicken once or twice during cooking.

Chicken Rolls

4 SERVINGS

2 chicken breasts, halved, skinned and boned
1 4-ounce can whole green chili peppers
4 teaspoon black olives, chopped and pitted
½ cup Monterey Jack cheese, shredded
1 egg, slightly beaten
1 cup tortilla chips, crushed
¼ cup vegetable oil
1 1.5-ounce envelope enchilada sauce mix
½ cup water
1 16-ounce can stewed tomatoes
½ cup cheddar cheese, shredded

Pre-heat oven to 350°F.

Pound chicken breasts to flatten. Place one chili pepper, 1 teaspoon chopped olives and 2 tablespoons Monterey Jack cheese on each chicken breast. Roll the breasts up tightly and secure with toothpicks.

Dip each chicken breast in egg, then in crushed chips to coat.

Heat oil in heavy skillet and brown rolls lightly.

Place rolls in a shallow casserole. Prepare enchilada sauce mix according to package directions, using water and tomatoes. Pour sauce over chicken rolls.

Bake for 35 to 40 minutes. Sprinkle cheddar cheese on top and bake an additional 5 minutes or until cheese is bubbly.

Mandarin-Onion Chicken

4 SERVINGS

1 cup long-grain rice, uncooked
2 large chicken breasts, halved and skinned
1 10 ½-ounce can mandarin oranges, drained and reserving juice
1 envelope dry onion soup mix

Pre-heat over to 350°F. Place rice in bottom of 9 x 13-inch oblong baking pan. Arrange chicken breasts on top of rice. Add water to reserved juice to make 1½ cups. Pour over chicken breasts and rice.

Arrange mandarin orange sections on top of chicken breasts and sprinkle with soup mix.

Cover with foil and bake for 1¼ hours or until chicken is tender.

DESSERTS

Fudge Brownies

32 1-INCH SQUARES

2 cups sugar
4 eggs
4 1-ounce squares bitter chocolate
2 sticks margarine or butter
1 1/2 cups flour
1 teaspoon vanilla
1 cup walnuts, chopped

Pre-heat oven to 350°F.

Beat sugar and eggs together. Melt chocolate squares and margarine in top of double boiler. Add to sugar and eggs.

Add flour and vanilla and blend well. Stir in nuts by hand.

Pour batter into 8 or 9-inch square baking pan and bake for 1 hour.

Apple Turnovers

12 PASTRIES

1 1/2 cups butter or margarine
4 cups flour
1/2 teaspoon salt
2 packages dry yeast
1 egg, beaten
Applesauce for filling

Pre-heat oven to 425°F.

Cut butter into flour and salt, until mixture looks like coarse cornmeal.

Dissolve yeast according to package directions. Mix yeast in beaten egg until all yeast is dissolved. Add to flour mixture. Knead thoroughly with hands. Roll out dough onto floured board. Cut with round cutter at least 3 inches in diameter.

Put 1 teaspoon of applesauce on half of each dough round. Fold over other half and seal edges with fork. Bake on greased baking sheet for 15 to 20 minutes. Glaze with favorite frosting when cold, if desired.

Caramel Custard

8 SERVINGS

5 eggs, beaten until foamy
1/3 cup sugar
1/4 teaspoon salt
3 cups milk
1 teaspoon vanilla extract
1/2 cup sugar, to caramelize
Ground nutmeg, to taste
Toasted almonds, to garnish

Pre-heat oven to 325°F. Set pan with 3/4-inch hot water in center of oven.

Stir sugar and salt into beaten eggs. Heat milk until just under boiling. Pour milk into egg mixture and continue to stir until sugar is dissolved. Add vanilla.

Melt sugar in small skillet over medium heat and stir until caramelized.

Pour caramelized sugar into 1 1/2-quart glass soufflé pan and add custard mixture. Sprinkle with nutmeg. Put casserole in pan of hot water and bake approximately 1 hour and 15 minutes. Remove from oven and chill.

To unmold, run spatula around edge and invert on serving plate. Caramel will form sauce.

To serve, sprinkle with toasted sliced almonds.

Chocolate Chip-Sour Cream Cake

1 9 × 13-INCH CAKE

1/4 pound butter or margarine
1 cup sugar
2 eggs
1 cup sour cream
1 teaspoon vanilla
2 cups flour
1 1/2 teaspoons baking powder
1 teaspoon baking soda
1/2 cup sugar
1 teaspoon cinnamon
2/3 cup chocolate chips

Pre-heat oven to 350°F.

Cream butter and sugar. Add eggs, sour cream, and vanilla and beat well. Sift together flour, baking powder, and baking soda. Add to creamed mixture.

Spread half the batter in greased and floured 9 × 13-inch pan. Combine sugar, cinnamon, and chocolate chips. Spread 3/4 of chip mixture on batter and press down chips. Repeat. Bake for 30 minutes.

Cider Cake

1 7 × 11 × 1-INCH CAKE

4 cups flour
3 teaspoons baking soda
1/4 teaspoon salt
1 teaspoon cinnamon
1 teaspoon allspice
1/2 cup shortening
4 eggs, separated
1 cup sugar
2 cups sweet cider
2 cups raisins

Pre-heat oven to 350°F. Grease a 7 × 11 × 1-inch baking pan and dust lightly with flour.

Sift flour, baking soda, salt and spices together.

Cream shortening until fluffy. Beat egg yolks until foamy. Gradually beat in sugar into shortening, then beat in egg yolks. Add flour mixture alternately with cider, beating well after each addition. Stir in raisins. Beat egg white stiffly and fold into batter. Pour into prepared pan and bake for 1 hour.

Fudge Cake

2 9-INCH LAYERS

4 squares unsweetened baking chocolate
1/2 cup hot water
1 3/4 cups sugar
2 cups cake flour
1 teaspoon baking soda
1 teaspoon salt
1/2 cup butter
3 eggs
2/3 cup milk
1 teaspoon vanilla

Pre-heat oven to 350°F. Grease two 9-inch layer pans and dust with flour.

Stir chocolate squares and water together in the top of a double boiler until chocolate melts. Add 1/2 cup sugar and stir together for 2 minutes. Set aside.

Sift cake flour, baking soda and salt together.

Cream butter, add remaining sugar and beat until light and fluffy. Add eggs, one at a time, beating well after each addition. Add flour mixture alternately with milk, beating after each addition of milk, until mixture is smooth. Stir in vanilla and melted chocolate.

Pour into prepared pans and bake for 20 minutes. Remove from pans after 10 minutes, cool and frost with a favorite frosting.

Gingersnaps

48 COOKIES

3/4 cup vegetable shortening
1 cup brown sugar
3/4 cup molasses
1 egg
2 1/4 cups flour
2 teaspoons baking soda
1/2 teaspoon salt
1 teaspoon ginger
1 teaspoon cinnamon
1/2 teaspoon cloves
Sugar, for coating

Pre-heat oven to 375°F. Grease cookie sheets.

Combine shortening, brown sugar, molasses and egg in a mixing bowl and beat until creamy.

Sift flour, baking soda, salt and spices together. Add to the creamed mixture and mix well.

Form dough into walnut-sized balls, roll in sugar to coat and place on greased cookie sheets 2 inches apart.

Bake for 10 minutes. Cool slightly and remove from cookie sheets to cooling trays.

Spicy Fruit Cookies

25 COOKIES

1 cup flour
1/4 teaspoon baking soda
1/4 teaspoon salt
1/2 teaspoon ginger
1/4 teaspoon cinnamon
1/4 teaspoon nutmeg
1 cup raisins
1 cup chopped walnuts
1/4 cup butter
1/4 cup brown sugar, firmly packed
2 eggs
1/4 teaspoon vanilla
1/2 cup molasses

Pre-heat oven to 350°F. Grease a shallow 9-inch square baking pan.

Sift flour, baking soda, salt and spices together. Stir in raisins and nuts.

Cream butter and sugar. Beat in eggs, one at a time, beating thoroughly after each addition. Stir in vanilla and molasses. Stir in flour mixture and mix well.

Pour into prepared pan and bake for 30 minutes. Cut into squares while warm.

Florentines

Florentines

APPROXIMATELY 30 COOKIES

¾ cup raisins
2 cups crushed cornflakes
¾ cup peanuts
½ cup maraschino cherries
½ can condensed milk
3 squares baking chocolate

Pre-heat oven to 375 F.
Grease 2 large baking sheets, line with greased paper, and dust lightly with cornstarch.
In large bowl, mix together raisins, cornflakes, peanuts, and cherries. Add condensed milk and blend well. Place 2 teaspoons of mixture in small heaps on baking sheets.
Bake for 15 to 20 minutes. Leave on baking sheets to cool. When cool, remove to trays.
Melt chocolate in double boiler, remove from heat, and stir until slightly thickened. Spread chocolate over flat side of cookie and mark with a fork. Allow chocolate to set before storing.

Corn Pudding

4 SERVINGS

2 tablespoons butter
2 tablespoons vegetable oil
½ onion, finely chopped
1 cup corn kernels
1 tablespoon sugar
Salt and pepper, to taste
3 eggs, separated
½ cup cheddar cheese

Pre-heat oven to 350°F.
Heat butter and oil in skillet and sauté onion. Stir in corn, sugar, salt, and pepper. Set aside to cool.
Beat egg yolks well, stir in cheese and add to cooled corn mixture.
Beat egg whites stiff and fold into corn-cheese mixture. Pour into well-greased 9 × 11 inch casserole. Set casserole in pan of hot water in oven. Bake for 1 hour. Serve immediately.

Peach Crisp

6 SERVINGS

1 10-ounce can sliced peaches
1/4 cup sugar
2 teaspoons lemon juice
3/4 cup flour, sifted
1/4 teaspoon salt
3/4 cups brown sugar, firmly packed
1/3 cup margarine

Pre-heat oven to 350°F.
Arrange sliced peaches in baking dish. Mix sugar and lemon juice together and spoon over peaches.
Combine flour, salt, and brown sugar. Cut in margarine until mixture is crumbly. Sprinkle over peaches. Bake for 50 to 55 minutes.
Serve warm, with vanilla ice cream, if desired.

Purple Plum Crunch

8 SERVINGS

5 cups fresh purple plums, pitted and quartered
1/4 cup brown sugar, firmly packed
3 tablespoons flour
1/2 teaspoon cinnamon
1 cup flour
1 cup sugar
1 teaspoon baking powder
1/2 teaspoon salt
1/2 teaspoon ground mace
1 egg, beaten
1/2 cup butter, melted
Topping:
1 8-ounce package cream cheese, beaten until fluffy
1 tablespoon confectioner's sugar, sifted
2 teaspoons orange rind, grated
1 tablespoons orange juice
2 tablespoons cream

Pre-heat oven to 375°F.
Place plums in bottom of ungreased, shallow, 2-quart baking dish. Mix brown sugar, 3 tablespoons flour, and cinnamon, and sprinkle over plums. Sift together 1 cup flour, sugar, baking powder, salt, and mace. Stir beaten egg into flour mixture. Stir together until mixture is crumbly. Sprinkle evenly over plums. Pour melted butter over all.
Bake for 40 to 50 minutes or until topping is lightly browned. To make topping, beat together cream cheese, confectioner's sugar, orange rind, orange juice, and cream.
Serve warm, with topping on the side.

Pumpkin Spice Cake

2 8-INCH CAKE LAYERS

2 1/2 cups sifted flour
1 teaspoon baking powder
1 teaspoon baking soda
1 teaspoon salt
3/4 teaspoon cinnamon
3/4 teaspoon cloves
1 cup granulated sugar
1/2 cup brown sugar, firmly packed
3/4 cup shortening, softened
1/2 cup buttermilk
1 1/2 cups pumpkin
3 eggs
1 cup whipping cream, whipped

Pre-heat oven to 350°F.
Sift together flour, baking powder, baking soda, salt, cinnamon, cloves, and sugar. Add brown sugar, shortening, buttermilk, and pumpkin. Beat for 2 minutes. Add eggs and beat for 2 additional minutes.
Pour batter into 2 greased and floured 8-inch cake pans. Bake for 30 to 35 minutes.
Cool cake for 5 minutes and remove from pan. Cool completely on cake rack.
To serve, spread at least 1/2 cup whipped cream over one layer; top with second layer. Garnish with additional whipped cream.

Bread Pudding

4 SERVINGS

1 1/2 cups (approximately 6 slices) bread, firmly packed
2 cups milk
3 eggs, lightly beaten
2 ripe bananas, sliced
1 apple, peeled and thinly sliced
1/2 cup raisins
1/2 cup sugar
1 1/2 teaspoons cinnamon
1 cup whipping cream
Vanilla, to taste
Sugar, to taste

Pre-heat oven to 350°F.
Soak bread in milk for 10 minutes. Mash mixture.
Add eggs, bananas, apple, raisins, cinnamon, and sugar. Pour mixture into buttered soufflé dish.
Place dish in pan of hot water in oven. Bake until knife inserted in center comes out clean, approximately 1 to 1 1/2 hours.
To serve, whip cream with vanilla and sugar. Top pudding with whipped cream when cool.

Sour Cream Coffee Cake

1 10-INCH TUBE CAKE

3 cups all-purpose flour, sifted
1 teaspoon salt
1/2 cup butter
3 egg yolks
1/4 cup sugar
1 cup sour cream
1 package dry yeast
1/4 cup lukewarm water
Melted butter, to spread
1/2 cup sugar combined with 1 teaspoon cinnamon
1/2 cup nuts, chopped
1/2 cup raisins

Place flour and salt in mixing bowl. Cut in butter. Beat egg yolks with sugar and add to flour mixture. Add sour cream. Dissolve yeast in lukewarm water and add to mixture. Blend well. Refrigerate overnight.
Roll out dough, spread with melted butter, sprinkle with sugar and cinnamon mixture, nuts, and raisins.
Roll up as a jelly roll and place around tube in a greased 10-inch tube pan. Cover and let rise in a warm place until dough doubles in size, approximately 2 hours.
Preheat oven to 350°F and bake for 40 to 55 minutes.

Blueberry Cake

12 SERVINGS

1 2/3 cups all-purpose flour
2 teaspoons baking powder
1/4 teaspoon salt
1/2 cup butter or margarine, softened
1 cup sugar
1 teaspoon vanilla extract
2 eggs
1/2 cup milk
1 cup blueberries
Confectioner's sugar, to garnish

Pre-heat oven to 350°F.
Combine flour, baking powder, and salt and set aside.
Cream butter or margarine, gradually adding sugar until light and fluffy. Stir in vanilla. Add eggs one at a time, beating well after each addition.
Add flour mixture alternately with milk, mixing just enough to blend after each addition. Fold in blueberries.
Pour batter into greased and floured 8 x 8 x 2-inch pan. Bake for 55 minutes.
To serve, dust with confectioner's sugar.

Coconut Custard Pie

1 9-INCH PIE

2 cups milk
4 eggs
1/2 cup flour
2/3 cup sugar
1 cup coconut
1/2 teaspoon salt
1 teaspoon vanilla extract

Pre-heat oven to 350°F, 325°F for glass pie pan. Blend together all ingredients. Pour into slightly greased 9-inch pie pan.
Bake for 50 minutes to 1 hour, until pie cracks on top.
Cool for 30 minutes before serving.

Apricot Upside-Down Cake

8 SERVINGS

Topping:
1/2 cup butter
1 cup brown sugar
1 1/2 cups apricots, cooked
1/2 cup raisins
1 tablespoon lemon juice
Batter:
1/2 cup butter
3/4 cup sugar
2 eggs
1 1/2 cups flour
1/8 teaspoon cloves
1/8 teaspoon salt
1 teaspoon baking soda
1/2 teaspoon cinnamon
1 cup sour cream
1 teaspoon vanilla extract

Pre-heat oven to 350°F.
To make topping, melt sugar and butter in a 10-inch heavy skillet. Arrange apricots and raisins in skillet. Sprinkle with lemon juice.
To make batter, cream together butter and sugar. Add eggs and mix well. Sift flour with cloves, salt, soda and cinnamon. Combine with creamed mixture, alternately with sour cream. Stir in vanilla.
Pour batter over apricots in skillet. Bake for 50 to 55 minutes, or until toothpick inserted in middle comes out clean.
To serve, turn out of skillet upside-down on cake platter.

American Homestead Winter

Winter

SOUPS & APPETIZERS

Cocktail Meatballs

12 SERVINGS

1 pound ground meat
Salt and pepper, to taste
Minced onions, to taste
Sauce:
½ cup catsup
½ cup water
3 bay leaves
2 tablespoons Worcestershire sauce
4 teaspoons vinegar
Juice of ½ lemon
4 tablespoons brown sugar
Pinch of dry mustard
1 ginger snap, crushed

Season ground meat with salt, pepper, and minced onions. Roll into small balls.

Combine remaining ingredients in a saucepan and simmer for 30 minutes. Add meat balls and simmer for 20 to 25 minutes. Remove bay leaves before serving.

Black Bean Soup

2 GALLONS

4 cups black beans, soaked overnight
½ cup butter
2 to 3 large onions, coarsely chopped
4 large garlic cloves, peeled and minced
4 leeks, coarsely chopped
2 celery ribs, coarsely chopped
2 bay leaves
2 or 3 cloves
16 cups veal or chicken stock
2 pounds smoked ham hocks
1 tablespoon salt
1 teaspoon black pepper
⅔ cup red wine
Hard-boiled eggs, chopped, to garnish
Parsley, chopped, to garnish
Lemon slices, to garnish

Drain beans in colander with pot underneath to catch the liquid.

Add water as needed to equal 3 quarts. Reserve.

Melt butter in large soup pot. Add onions, garlic, leeks, celery, bay leaves, and cloves. Sauté vegetables for 5 to 7 minutes.

Add veal stock, bean water, beans, ham hocks, salt, and pepper. Bring to a boil, then simmer for 3 hours with soup pot partially covered.

Remove ham hocks and cool. Strip meat and reserve. Puree soup by batches through food mill or in blender. Pour into clean soup pot. Taste and adjust seasoning; add reserved ham meat and wine. Bring to a boil. Remove from heat and ladle into serving bowls.

Serve with chopped eggs, chopped parsley, and lemon slices on the side.

Cheese Straws

12 SERVINGS

⅔ cup butter
2 cups cheddar cheese, grated
¼ teaspoon cayenne pepper
8 tablespoons ice water
2 cups flour
2 tablespoons sugar
Salt, to taste

Pre-heat oven to 350°F.

Combine all ingredients and mix until dough forms. Roll out to ¼ inch thickness on floured surface. Cut into strips ¼ inch x 5 inches. Bake 10 minutes or until golden brown.

Lima Bean Soup

1 GALLON

1 2-pound package large lima beans, soaked according to package directions
5 quarts water
1 whole onion
3 carrots, chopped
3 ribs celery, halved
1½ pound chuck roast, with bones
3 medium potatoes, cubed
Salt and pepper, to taste

Wash lima beans in hot water and drain. Bring water to boil in large soup pot. Add remaining ingredients. Bring to a boil again, reduce heat and simmer for 3 hours or until beans are tender.

New England Fish Chowder

8 SERVINGS

2½ pounds haddock fillets
2 cups water
½ cup butter
1¾ cups onions, thinly sliced
3 tablespoons flour
2½ cups potatoes, peeled and cubed
2 cups celery, coarsely chopped
1 bay leaf
2½ teaspoons salt
¼ teaspoon pepper
4 cups milk
1 cup medium cream
1 cup sour cream

Simmer fish in water in large pan for 5 minutes or until fish flakes. Remove fish and set aside to cool. Boil fish broth for 10 minutes until reduced to approximately 1⅔ cups. Remove skin from cooled fish.

Sauté onions in 5 tablespoons butter for 5 minutes. Remove from heat. Stir in flour and gradually add fish broth. Add potatoes, celery, seasonings and three-quarters of cooled fish. Simmer for 20 minutes or until potatoes are tender.

Scald milk. Remove from heat and add cream and sour cream. Beat with wire whisk or beater until sour cream is well-blended. Reheat slowly; do not boil. Add potato mixture and remaining fish. Heat for 5 minutes. Remove bay leaf. Dot with remaining butter. Soup is best when made a day or two before serving.

Shrimp Toast

12 SERVINGS

12 slices white bread, crusts trimmed
1 pound shrimp, peeled and deveined
¼ cup onion, finely chopped
2 teaspoons salt
1 teaspoon sugar
1 tablespoon cornstarch
½ teaspoon monosodium glutamate
1 egg, beaten
1 6-ounce can water chestnuts, drained and finely
*   chopped*
Oil, to deep-fry
Parsley, chopped, to garnish

Dry bread slices slightly.

Chop shrimp very fine in blender. Toss shrimp with onion, salt, sugar, cornstarch, and monosodium glutamate, mixing well. Spread mixture on bread slices and cut each into quarters.

In large, heavy skillet or saucepan, heat approximately 1 inch of oil to 375°F. Drop bread pieces, several at a time, shrimp side down, in hot oil. Deep-fry until edges of bread begin to brown. Turn on other side; fry until golden brown.

Remove with a slotted spoon and drain well on paper towels. Sprinkle with chopped parsley. Serve warm. Shrimp Toast can be made in advance and reheated in a 375°F. oven for 10 minutes.

Quiche Tarts

24 TARTS

1 package crescent rolls
1⅓ cups Swiss cheese, shredded
⅔ cup bacon, crumbled
⅓ cup chives
4 eggs, slightly beaten
1⅓ cups sour cream
1 teaspoon salt
1 teaspoon Worcestershire sauce

Pre-heat oven to 375°F.

Roll out crescent rolls until thin. Cut into 3-inch rounds. Place in muffin tin cups.

Combine cheese, bacon, and chives. Place 1 tablespoon of mixture on each dough round.

Combine eggs, sour cream, salt, and Worcestershire sauce. Pour into each tin until almost full.

Bake for 20 to 25 minutes. These can be prepared in advance and frozen.

Chestnut Soup

4 SERVINGS

1 quart chestnuts
4 cups water
1 tablespoon lemon rind, chopped
1 teaspoon parsley, chopped
1 teaspoon salt
4 cups chicken stock
1 tablespoon butter
1 tablespoon flour
2 egg yolks, beaten
Croutons, to garnish

Boil chestnuts for 15 minutes. Shell, remove skins, and chop finely. Place in soup pot. Add water, lemon rind, parsley, and salt. Bring to a boil, reduce heat, cover and simmer for 30 minutes.

Remove from heat and cool slightly. Puree mixture and return to soup pot. Add stock and bring to a boil. Blend butter and flour to a smooth paste. Add to soup, stirring constantly until mixed. Cover and simmer for 30 minutes, stirring occasionally.

Pour beaten egg yolks in tureen. Pour in soup. Garnish with croutons before serving.

Cream of Sorrel Soup

8 SERVINGS

½ pound sorrel
2 spring onions, chopped
1 tablespoon butter
3 cups chicken stock
2 egg yolks
4 tablespoons heavy cream
Salt, to taste
Minced chives or parsley, to garnish

Wash sorrel and discard tough stems and wilted leaves; chop. Sauté sorrel and onions briefly in butter until onions are transparent.

Add chicken stock and simmer, covered, for 10 minutes. Cool slightly and puree soup in blender or food processor.

Beat together egg yolks and cream. Add ½ cup of hot chicken stock in a thin stream to egg mixture.

Stir egg mixture and remaining stock into soup and barely simmer. Do not allow to boil. Remove from heat. Salt to taste, and refrigerate.

Serve when cold, garnish with a sprinkling of minced chives or parsley.

The Old Oaken Bucket

Squash Soup

4 SERVINGS

1 large squash
3/8 cup margarine
1 onion, peeled and sliced
1 cup water
Bouquet garni
Salt and pepper, to taste
3 tablespoons flour
1 cup milk
1 egg yolk
2 tablespoons evaporated milk

Peel squash, remove seeds and dice.

Melt margarine in a large saucepan. Sauté squash and onion slices in margarine for 5 minutes, stirring well.

Add water, bouquet garni, salt and pepper. Simmer until squash is very soft. Remove bouquet garni and cool slightly.

Puree mixture in food processor or blender and return to saucepan.

Blend flour and milk and stir into saucepan, stirring constantly.

Heat squash mixture to boiling. Reduce heat and simmer for 5 minutes.

Mix egg yolk and evaporated milk together. Pour in a thin stream into squash soup, stirring constantly. Heat soup through, but do not boil. Adjust seasonings before serving.

American Farm Scene No. 4

Ham Appetizer

4 SERVINGS

2 tablespoons green pepper, finely chopped
2 tablespoons celery, finely chopped
2 tablespoons pimento, finely chopped
¼ teaspoon Dijon mustard
2 teaspoons lemon juice
2 teaspoons olive oil
Salt and pepper, to taste
4 slices cooked ham
Stuffed olives or gherkins, to garnish

Mix green pepper, celery, and pimento together. Mix mustard with lemon juice and oil. Add salt and pepper to taste. Pour over vegetables and mix well.
Divide mixture equally on four slices of ham. Fold ham over mixture and secure with toothpicks.
Arrange on a serving platter and garnish with stuffed olives or gherkins cut into fan shapes.

Curried Tomato-Navy Bean Soup

8 SERVINGS

4 tablespoons butter
1½ cups onion, minced
3 cloves garlic, minced
1 tablespoon curry powder
3 pounds tomatoes, quartered
4 cups chicken broth
1 pound navy beans, soaked overnight and cooked
     according to package directions
1½ cups seasoned bread crumbs
Salt and pepper, to taste

Sauté onions and garlic in butter. Add curry and cook for 2 minutes. Add tomatoes, broth, and pre-cooked beans. Simmer for 30 minutes. Add bread crumbs and season with salt and pepper to taste.

Broccoli Chowder

6 SERVINGS

2 pounds fresh broccoli
4 cups chicken broth
3 cups milk
1 cup cooked ham, chopped
2 teaspoons salt
1/4 teaspoon pepper
1 cup half-and-half cream
2 cups Swiss cheese, shredded
1/4 cup butter
1/3 cup parsley, chopped

Combine broccoli and 2 cups chicken broth in large soup pot. Cover and cook for 7 minutes or until broccoli is crisp but tender. Remove broccoli from broth; cool and chop coarsely.

Add remaining chicken broth, milk, ham, salt, and pepper. Simmer over medium heat, stirring occasionally, for 5 minutes.

Stir in broccoli, cream, Swiss chess, butter and parsley. Simmer for 5 minutes. Do not allow to boil.

Butternut Squash and Apple Soup

12 SERVINGS

1 small butternut squash, about 1 pound
3 tart green apples
1 medium onion, coarsely chopped
1/4 teaspoon rosemary
1/4 teaspoon marjoram
6 cups chicken broth
4 cups water
2 slices white bread, crumbled
Salt and pepper, to taste
1/4 cup heavy cream
2 tablespoons parsley, chopped

Halve squash, peel, dice and seed. Peel, core and chop apples. Combine squash and apples with onion, rosemary, marjoram, broth, water, bread, salt, and pepper in soup pot. Bring to a boil and simmer, uncovered, for 45 minutes.

Puree soup, a batch at a time, in blender. Return to soup pot and bring to a boil. Ladle into serving bowls. To serve, add heavy cream, and garnish with sprinkling of chopped parsley.

Chicken Corn Soup

8 SERVINGS

1 2 1/2 pound chicken
4 cups water
2 teaspoons salt
1/4 teaspoon pepper
Pinch of saffron
2 cups corn kernels
1 cup celery, chopped
1 tablespoon parsley, chopped

Put chicken in large soup pot. Cover with water. Add salt, pepper, and saffron. Bring to a boil and simmer until tender. Cool chicken enough to handle. Remove skin from meat and debone. Cut into bite-size pieces. Measure 2 cups of chicken. Save remainder to use at another time.

Bring 4 cups of broth to a boil. Add corn, celery, and parsley. Boil for 5 minutes. Add chicken. Season to taste.

Cream of Potato Soup

6 SERVINGS

3 tablespoons butter
4 medium potatoes, pared and chopped
2 medium onions, peeled and chopped
2 ribs celery, chopped
2 1/2 cups boiling water
1 bay leaf
4 sprigs parsley
1/8 teaspoon thyme
Salt and pepper, to taste
1/4 teaspoon mace or nutmeg
2 cups milk, scalded
1 cup whipping cream, to garnish
Chopped chives or parsley, to garnish

Melt the butter in a large saucepan. Sauté the potatoes, onions, and celery stirring frequently, for 5-6 minutes. Add boiling water and mix well. Add herbs, salt and pepper, and mace or nutmeg. Bring to a boil. Reduce heat, and simmer, covered, for 30-40 minutes, or until vegetables are tender. Stir occasionally.

Remove bay leaf. Puree soup mixture in a blender or food processor. Reheat pureed soup. Add scalded milk.

Adjust seasoning to taste.

To serve, garnish with a spoonful of cream, a sprinkling of chopped chives or parsley. Serve with cheese croutons.

VEGETABLES & SALADS

Vegetable Nut Salad

8 SERVINGS

2 heads leaf lettuce
2 cucumbers, peeled and thinly sliced
1 pound mixed nuts, coarsely chopped
1/2 pound bean sprouts
2 red peppers, diced
4 scallions, diced
2 green peppers, diced
3 carrots, grated
4 tomatoes, cut in wedges
1 5³/4 ounce can large black olives, pitted and drained

Line 1 large or 8 individual salad bowls with lettuce. Build salad in layers, beginning with layer of cucumbers, then nuts, bean sprouts, red peppers, nuts, scallions, green peppers, nuts, and carrots.

Arrange tomato wedges and black olives on top and sprinkle lightly with remaining chopped nuts. Refrigerate.

Serve cold accompanied by preferred dressing.

Carrot Ring

8 SERVINGS

1¹/2 cups butter
³/4 cups brown sugar
3 eggs
1¹/2 cups raw carrots, grated
2¹/4 cups cake flour
³/4 teaspoon baking soda
2 tablespoons plus 2 teaspoons hot water

Pre-heat oven to 325°F.
Cream butter and brown sugar together, beating well. Add eggs and cream again. Stir in grated carrots.
Sift cake flour and baking soda together. Add to carrot mixture with water.
Pout into a greased 10-inch tube pan. Bake for 1 hour.

Broccoli Fritters

8 SERVINGS

2 9-ounce packages frozen chopped broccoli, cooked
1/2 cup butter
1 cup water
Salt, to taste
Pinch of garlic powder
1 cup flour, sifted
4 eggs
Vegetable oil, to deep-fry
1/2 cup Parmesan cheese, grated

Combine butter, water, salt, and garlic powder in large saucepan. Heat until water is boiling and butter melts. Add flour all at once. Remove from heat.
Stir mixture quickly with wooden spoon until dough comes away from side of pan and forms mound in center. Add eggs one at a time, beating well after each addition until mixture is smooth. Stir broccoli into dough. Chill 2 hours or overnight.
Pour oil into deep skillet or large saucepan to depth of 3 inches. Heat to 375°F.
Scoop up teaspoon of dough and carefully push into oil with another teaspoon. Fry a small batch at a time. Brown on one side approximately 2 minutes; turn and brown other side. Remove with slotted spoon and drain.
Sprinkle with Parmesan cheese and serve immediately.

Cabbage Noodles

4 SERVINGS

1 head cabbage, quartered
2 large onions, sliced
1 cup butter or margarine
Salt and pepper, to taste
1/2 pound broad noodles

Soak cabbage quarters in cold, salted water for 5 minutes. Drain and grate coarsely. Cover, and set aside 30 minutes.
In a large skillet, sauté onions in 2 tablespoons butter or margarine until golden brown.
Press remaining water from cabbage. Add cabbage, salt, and pepper to onions. Simmer, uncovered, adding butter or margarine as needed, for approximately 1 hour. Stir occasionally to avoid sticking.
Prepare noodles according to package directions and drain. Mix with browned, seasoned cabbage and serve immediately.

American Forest Scene—Maple Sugaring

Winter in the Country

Broccoli and Cheddar Cheese Casserole

8 SERVINGS

2 cups onion, minced
3 tablespoons butter
1 tablespoon vegetable oil
2¹/₂ cups broccoli, peeled, chopped, and blanched
1 cup cheese, grated
1 cup table cream
Pinch of salt
Pinch of pepper
Pinch of nutmeg
8 large eggs, beaten

Pre-heat oven to 350°F.

Sauté onion in butter and oil until tender. Stir in broccoli and cook for 5 minutes.

In large bowl, combine cheese, cream, and broccoli mixture. Add salt, pepper, and nutmeg. Fold beaten eggs into mixture.

Pour into 6-cup baking dish which has been lined with buttered parchment paper.

Set dish in large pan filled with boiling water; bake for 45 minutes, or until custard is set.

Remove baking dish from oven and water. Let dish set 20 minutes before unmolding.

Hot Potato Salad

6 SERVINGS

6 medium potatoes
1/2 cup French dressing
1 cup butter
1 tablespoon flour
1/2 cup milk
1/2 cup mayonnaise
1 onion, finely chopped

Boil potatoes in skin. Cool slightly, then cut into slices or cubes. Marinate in French dressing for 8 hours.

Melt butter in a heavy saucepan. Remove from heat and whisk in flour. Return to heat and simmer butter-flour mixture for 1 minute. Whisk in milk, stirring constantly. Bring mixture to a boil, reduce heat and stir constantly until mixture thickens.

Pre-heat oven to 400°F.

Mix mayonnaise, onion and white sauce. Stir into potatoes. Place in a 4-quart casserole and bake, uncovered, for 30 minutes. Serve warm.

Turkey Stuffed Tomatoes

4 SERVINGS

4 large tomatoes
1/2 cucumber
2 ribs celery
4 tablespoons canned corn
1/2 cup mayonnaise
1 cup cooked turkey, chopped
4 slices lemon, to garnish
Chopped parsley, to garnish

Cut off tops of tomatoes, remove insides and reserve juice. Peel cucumber, dice and sprinkle with salt. Set aside for 20 minutes. Wash, drain and chop celery and mix with corn.

Combine mayonnaise and juice from tomatoes.

Combine vegetables and turkey. Stir in mayonnaise.

Fill tomatoes with vegetable–turkey mixture. Garnish with sliced lemon and chopped parsley. Serve with brown bread and butter.

Green Beans with Cheese

6 SERVINGS

1/4 cup butter or margarine
1/2 cup seasoned bread crumbs
2 tablespoons flour
1 teaspoon salt
1/4 teaspoon pepper
1/4 teaspoon onion, minced
1 teaspoon sugar
1 cup sour cream
4 cups French cut green beans, cooked and drained
2 cups Swiss cheese, grated

Pre-heat oven to 400°F.

Melt 2 tablespoons of butter in small saucepan. Remove from heat. Add bread crumbs. Mix well and set aside.

Melt remaining 2 tablespoons of butter in large saucepan over low heat. Stir in flour, salt, pepper, onion, and sugar. Add sour cream. Stir until smooth. Increase heat to medium and cook until sauce is bubbly and thickened, stirring constantly. Remove from heat.

Fold green beans into sour cream sauce. Spread in greased 1½-quart baking dish. Sprinkle cheese evenly over green bean mixture. Sprinkle crumb mixture evenly over cheese.

Bake for 20 minutes or until thoroughly heated. Other vegetables can be substituted for green beans.

FISH & SEAFOOD

Cippino Fish Stew

6 SERVINGS

1 8-ounce can whole kernel corn
1 16-ounce can tomatoes, chopped
1/4 teaspoon oregano, crumbled
1 pound 1/2-inch thick fish fillets
1/3 cup teriyaki sauce
2 ribs celery, chopped
1/8 teaspoon Tabasco sauce

Drain corn and reserve liquid. Combine liquid with tomatoes and oregano in medium saucepan and bring to a boil. Cover, reduce heat, and simmer 15 minutes.

Cut fish into 1½-inch pieces and marinate in teriyaki sauce for 10 minutes.

Add fish, teriyaki sauce and celery to tomato mixture in saucepan and simmer 10 additional minutes.

Stir in corn and Tabasco sauce and simmer 5 minutes or until fish flakes easily with a fork. Serve immediately.

Oven Halibut Steaks

6 SERVINGS

2 pounds halibut steaks
1 cup dry bread crumbs
1 teaspoon salt
1/8 teaspoon pepper
1/2 teaspoon paprika
1/4 cup melted butter

Pre-heat oven to 450°F.

Cut halibut into serving portions. Combine bread crumbs with salt, pepper and paprika. Dip steaks in melted butter, then dip in crumb mixture.

Place on well-oiled baking sheet. Bake approximately 12 minutes or until fish flakes with a fork.

Cajun Crabcakes

4 SERVINGS

1 large egg, beaten
1 tablespoon mayonnaise
Salt, to taste
1/4 teaspoon ground black pepper
1/4 teaspoon curry powder
3 to 4 drops hot pepper sauce
1 teaspoon Worcestershire sauce
1 tablespoon fresh lemon juice
1/8 teaspoon ground cloves
1/8 teaspoon cayenne
1/2 teaspoon paprika
1/4 teaspoon dry mustard
1/4 teaspoon celery salt
1 pound jumbo lump crabmeat, cartilage removed
3 to 4 tablespoons dry bread crumbs
2 cups vegetable oil

Combine egg, mayonnaise and seasonings. Add crabmeat and enough bread crumbs to absorb excess moisture.

Stir to blend well. Mixture should be firm enough to hold together. Adjust seasonings.

Form crabmeat mixture into eight patties. Place on wax paper for about 20 minutes to dry slightly.

Heat 1-inch of oil in a heavy skillet to 350°F. Fry crabcakes 3 to 4 minutes each side or until golden brown. Do not crowd pan. Drain on paper towels and serve immediately.

Salmon with Parsley Sauce

6 SERVINGS

1 pound salmon fillets
Salt and pepper, to taste
2 tablespoons butter
2 tablespoons olive oil
1 1/4 cups green onions, thinly sliced
1 cup fresh parsley, chopped
3/4 dry white wine or water

Season salmon to taste.

Heat butter and olive oil in a heavy skillet. Sauté onion and ½ cup parsley until onion is transparent. Add wine or water and simmer for 2 minutes.

Add salmon fillets, and simmer, covered, 4 to 5 minutes, or until salmon is opaque and just flakes.

Stir in remaining parsley and adjust seasonings to taste.

To serve, pour over hot pasta and gently toss.

American Winter Sports

The Road—Winter

Lobster with Chicken and Tomatoes

8 SERVINGS

4 chicken breasts, skinned and split
1½ teaspoons salt
¼ teaspoon pepper
½ cup butter or margarine
2 tablespoons sherry
½ pound mushrooms, sliced
2 tablespoons flour
1½ cups chicken broth
1 tablespoon tomato paste
1 bay leaf, crushed
2 tablespoons fresh chives, chopped
1 pound lobster meat
3 ripe tomatoes, peeled and quartered

Pre-heat oven to 350°F.

Sprinkle chicken breasts with salt and pepper. Heat butter until foamy. Add chicken breasts and sauté until golden. Spoon sherry over chicken. Remove from skillet and place in shallow baking dish, cover with foil, and bake for 25 to 30 minutes, until tender.

Add mushrooms to skillet and sauté until tender. Blend flour into butter in skillet; add chicken broth and simmer, stirring constantly, until thickened. Season with tomato paste, bay leaf, chives, salt, and pepper.

Remove lobster meat from shell; cut into bite-size pieces. Add lobster meat to sauce along with tomatoes. Simmer 5 to 8 minutes, until lobster and tomatoes are just heated.

Serve chicken breasts on platter topped with sauce, arranging tomatoes and lobster meat around chicken.

Lobster Ramekins

8 SERVINGS

½ cup butter
1 pound lobster meat
1 cup celery hearts, finely diced
4 tablespoons shallots, finely minced
2 cups fresh mushrooms, washed and sliced
¼ cup dry white wine or water
1 teaspoon seafood seasoning
2 teaspoons fresh thyme
1½ tablespoons flour
¾ cup light cream
Lemon twist, to garnish
Chopped parsley, to garnish

Melt butter over low heat in a skillet. Do not allow butter to brown or boil. Cut the lobster meat into small chunks. Sauté the lobster chunks in butter until heated through. Avoid breaking up the lobster chunks.

Add celery, shallots, mushrooms, wine or water, seafood seasoning and thyme. Heat mixture thoroughly, stirring gently.

Gently press the liquid from the lobster mixture and divide lobster between 8 1-cup ramekins. Leave ¼ cup lobster liquid in the skillet, or add more butter to make ¼ cup liquid.

Sprinkle the flour over the butter and whisk into a thin paste. Add the cream while whisking. Simmer, stirring constantly, until sauce thickens.

Pour sauce over lobster ramekins. Garnish with a lemon twist and chopped parsley. Serve warm.

Tuna Fried Rice

4 to 6 SERVINGS

1 cup long-grain rice
1 medium onion, thinly sliced
2 tablespoons vegetable oil
*1 10-ounce package oriental-style vegetables with
    seasoning sauce, thawed*
1 2-ounce jar pimentos
2 tablespoons soy sauce
1 7-ounce can tuna, drained

Prepare rice according to package directions.

Sauté onion in oil over medium heat in 12-inch skillet or wok until transparent, about 5 minutes.

Stir in cooked rice and thawed vegetables, stir and cook for 5 minutes.

Carefully stir in pimentos, soy sauce and tuna, being careful not to break up tuna chunks.

Serve with additional soy sauce.

Papiotte

2 SERVINGS

2 6 to 8-ounce flounder fillets
Salt and pepper, to taste
4 tablespoons cream of celery soup
4 tablespoons water
½ cup small mushrooms, washed and drained
Dry mustard, to taste
Nutmeg, to taste

Pre-heat oven to 400°F.

Place each flounder fillet in center of a 1 foot square of aluminum foil. Sprinkle with salt and pepper.

Blend soup and water with mushrooms, mustard and nutmeg and pour over fish fillets.

Bring two sides of foil together and fold over twice. Turn ends up so juice can't escape. Place on a baking sheet and bake 20 to 30 minutes, or until fish flakes easily with a fork.

Tuna with Mushrooms

4 SERVINGS

1½ pounds skinless tuna, cut into 1-inch steaks
2 teaspoons minced garlic
1 cup onions, sliced
2 tablespoons olive oil
½ cup carrots, julienned
*1 16-ounce can whole tomatoes, drained and coarsely
    chopped*
2 tablespoons fresh parsley, chopped
¼ teaspoon fennel seeds
½ bay leaf
¼ cup orange juice
½ teaspoon orange rind, grated

Rinse tuna steaks with cold water. Pat dry.

In a Dutch oven, sauté garlic and onions in olive oil until onions are transparent. Stir in carrots, tomatoes, 1 tablespoon parsley, fennel, bay leaf and orange juice. Cover and simmer for 5 minutes.

Place fish steaks on top of tomato mixture in a single layer. Cover Dutch oven and simmer for approximately 8 minutes. Tuna steaks should be opaque on the outside, but slightly pink in the center when removed from the heat.

Season with salt and pepper if desired. Remove to serving platter and garnish with remaining parsley and grated orange rind.

MEATS

Ham, Apple and Sweet Potato Casserole

4 SERVINGS

1 center slice ham
3 medium sweet potatoes, sliced ¼ inch thick
4 apples, quartered
2 tablespoons sugar
¾ cup hot water

Pre-heat oven to 350°F.

Brown ham slightly on both sides and place in a baking dish.

Spread sweet potatoes and apples over ham and sprinkle with sugar. Add hot water.

Cover and bake until tender, about 1 hour. Baste occasionally. Remove cover last 15 minutes to brown casserole.

Veal Loaf

4 SERVINGS

2 pounds ground veal
1 medium onion, chopped
½ green pepper, seeded and finely chopped
1 tablespoon red wine vinegar
2 teaspoons Worcestershire sauce
½ teaspoon salt
½ cup cracker crumbs
1 15-ounce can thick and chunky tomato sauce
Green olives, with pimento centers, sliced, to garnish

Pre-heat oven to 350°F.

Combine veal, onion, pepper, vinegar, Worcestershire sauce, salt, cracker crumbs and ½ cup tomato sauce. Press mixture in a loaf pan and garnish with olives.

Cover with foil and bake for 40 minutes. Uncover and bake for 15 to 20 minutes longer, or until browned on top. Remove from oven and let stand for 5 to 10 minutes. Unmold from pan.

To serve, slice into 1-inch thick pieces and garnish with remaining tomato sauce.

Spanish Steak

8 SERVINGS

2¼ pound round steak
2 teaspoons salt
⅛ teaspoon pepper
½ cup flour
2 tablespoons butter
1 6-ounce can tomato paste
¾ cup water
½ cup green pepper, seeded and chopped
⅓ cup onion, chopped
Gravy:
1 tablespoon flour
1 8-ounce package cream cheese

Cut meat into serving pieces. Sprinkle with salt and pepper. Coat meat with flour and score with a sharp knife. Coat again with flour.

Melt butter in a heavy skillet and brown meat slowly on all sides.

Combine tomato paste, water, green pepper and onion. Pour over meat. Cover and simmer over low heat 1½ to 2 hours, or until meat is fork-tender.

Transfer meat to a warmed platter.

To make gravy, whisk flour into pan drippings. Simmer, stirring constantly, until thickened, about 5 minutes. Remove from heat and stir in cream cheese. Immediately pour gravy over steak and serve.

Lamb Swiss Steak

4 SERVINGS

1½ cups cracker crumbs
2 teaspoons dry mustard
½ teaspoon salt
1 egg
⅓ cup milk
4 lamb steaks, cut 1-inch thick
½ cup melted shortening

Combine cracker crumbs, mustard and salt. In a second bowl, beat together egg and milk.

Dip lamb steaks in egg mixture until coated, then dip in cracker mixture, covering both sides well with crumbs.

Place breaded steaks on wax paper and chill for 15 minutes.

Heat shortening in heavy skillet. Sauté lamb steaks about 7 minutes on each side. Cover and simmer over low heat for about 15 minutes, or until lamb is tender.

Beef Roll

Beef Roll

6 SERVINGS

Filling:
1 tablespoon vegetable oil
1 pound ground beef
1 onion, peeled and chopped
1/2 cup chopped mushrooms
1 teaspoon salt
1/4 teaspoon freshly ground black pepper
1/4 teaspoon dry mustard
1/4 cup chopped olives
2 tablespoons finely chopped parsley
1 1/4 cups beef gravy
Pastry:
1 3/4 cups all-purpose flour
1 teaspoon salt
2 1/2 teaspoons baking powder
3 tablespoons finely chopped parsley
1/3 cup shortening
Approximately 2/3 cup milk

Pre-heat oven to 400°F.

Heat oil in skillet, add meat, onion, and mushrooms and sauté, stirring frequently, until meat and onion are brown. Stir in all the seasonings, olives, parsley, and 1/4 cup of gravy to moisten. Stir together over low heat for 5 minutes, then let cool while making the pastry.

Sift together flour, salt, and baking powder. Add parsley. Cut in shortening until mixture resembles bread crumbs. Add enough milk to make a soft dough. Turn onto a floured surface and knead lightly.

Roll into an oblong shape about 10 by 14 inches. Spread meat mixture over dough to within 1/2 inch of the edges. Dampen edges of pastry and roll up like a jelly roll, pressing the edges together well.

Place roll on greased baking sheet and bake for approximately 30 minutes. Serve hot, cut into slices, with the remaining gravy, or cold with a salad.

Casserole of Beef with Walnuts

6 SERVINGS

2 tablespoons peanut oil
1½ to 2 pounds beef chuck
1 tablespoon flour
12 small white onions, peeled
¼ cup red wine
1 teaspoon bouquet garni
1 garlic clove, slivered
1½ to 2 cups beef bouillon stock
1 small stalk celery, about ½ pound
1 tablespoon butter or margarine
¼ cup walnut meats
Pinch of salt
Rind of ½ orange, shredded and blanched, to garnish

Pre-heat oven to 325°F.

Heat 1 tablespoon oil in saucepan and brown meat. Sprinkle in flour and cook for 3 to 5 minutes. Remove from saucepan and set aside.

Sauté onions in remaining oil until they begin to color, and then add to meat. Transfer meat and onions to casserole; pouring off excess fat first, reserving 1 tablespoon in saucepan. Add wine, bouquet garni, garlic, and 1½ cups bouillon to saucepan. Stir until boiling; pour over casserole. Add extra bouillon stock, if necessary, to cover meat. Season to taste. Simmer slowly for approximately 2 hours.

Trim celery and cut into strips. Heat butter, add celery, walnut meats, and a pinch of salt. Stir over heat for several minutes. When ready to serve, scatter celery, walnut meats, and orange rind over meat.

Casserole of Beef with Walnuts

Lamb Stew

4 SERVINGS

2 pounds lamb, cut in 2-inch cubes
1 large onion, diced
¼ cup dry white wine
2 cups chicken stock
2 tablespoons butter
8 small white onions, peeled
10 small potatoes, peeled
2 ribs celery, diced
4 small leeks, white part only, diced
4 small turnips, peeled
Flour, to thicken
Salt and pepper, to taste
Parsley, to garnish
Paprika, to garnish

Trim excess fat and gristle from lamb. Make bed of diced onion in a heavy skillet. Top with lamb in single layer. Add wine and 1 cup chicken stock. Cover, bring liquid to boil rapidly, reduce heat, and simmer gently until meat is tender, approximately 1 hour.

Strain, reserving stock. If desired, refrigerate meat in stock overnight.

Melt butter in skillet, add white onions, cover, and simmer for 10 minutes. Add remaining vegetables and stock and simmer until tender, approximately 25 minutes.

Strain and combine broth with reserved stock. To thicken, allow 2 tablespoons flour for each cup of stock. Season to taste, stirring constantly until thickened.

Arrange lamb in center of serving platter. Arrange row of vegetables along each side and spread with thickened sauce. Sprinkle vegetables with parsley and lamb with paprika.

Persian Lamb Chops

6 SERVINGS

6 lamb chops, cut 1-inch thick
2 tablespoons lemon juice
Paprika, to taste
Salt and pepper, to taste
1 cup yogurt
1/2 cup onion, finely chopped
1 garlic clove, minced

Place lamb chops in glass baking dish. Sprinkle with lemon juice and allow to stand for a few minutes. Sprinkle generously with paprika, salt and pepper. Combine yogurt, onion and garlic and pour over lamb chops. Refrigerate for 8 hours.
Pre-heat broiler.
Broil lamb chops to desired doneness.

Sauerbraten

8 to 10 SERVINGS

4 pound boneless beef chuck or rump
2/3 cup teriyaki sauce
2 cups vinegar
2 cups water
1/3 cup sugar
1 medium onion, sliced
1 teaspoon peppercorns
4 bay leaves
2 tablespoons vegetable oil

Place meat in bowl or crock. Add teriyaki sauce and marinate for 30 minutes.
Heat vinegar, water and sugar to boiling, remove from heat and cool slightly.
Arrange onion, peppercorns and bay leaves over meat. Pour vinegar mixture over meat. Cover tightly and refrigerate 3 to 4 days, turning meat occasionally. Remove meat and drain well. Reserve 1 cup marinade.
Pre-heat oven to 300°F.
Heat oil in Dutch oven, add meat and brown well on all sides. Add reserved marinade. Cover and roast for 3 hours or until beef is tender.
To serve, spoon pan juices over meat, or thicken juices with 2 tablespoons flour mixed with 1 tablespoon of water and 2 crumbled gingersnaps and pour over meat.

Curried Lamb Stew

4 SERVINGS

2 pounds lamb stew meat, cut into 1-inch cubes
4 tablespoons vegetable oil
4 tablespoons flour
1/2 teaspoon curry powder
1 cup chicken bouillon
1 cup water
1 cup celery, chopped
1 medium onion, thinly sliced
1 medium apple, finely chopped
1 garlic clove, minced
1 teaspoon salt
1/4 teaspoon pepper

Heat oil in heavy saucepan. Brown lamb, then remove.
Add flour and curry powder to lamb drippings in saucepan and blend well.
Gradually stir in bouillon and water. Add remaining ingredients and cook over low heat, stirring constantly until thickened.
Return lamb to saucepan. Cover and simmer for 1½ hours.
Serve over rice.

Oriental Pork Roast

6 SERVINGS

1 4-pound pork loin roast
3/4 cup soy sauce
1/3 cup water
1/3 cup honey
2 garlic cloves, crushed
1/2 teaspoon ginger

Pierce roast all over with a fork and place in a large plastic bag. Combine soy sauce, water, honey, garlic and ginger and pour over roast in bag. Press air out of bag and fasten securely. Refrigerate 8 hours, turning bag occasionally.
Pre-heat oven to 325°F.
Remove roast from plastic bag, reserving marinade. Place roast in a shallow roasting pan. Roast for 1 hour. Remove roast from oven and brush with reserved marinade. Cover with aluminum foil and roast for an additional 1½ hours, brushing several times with reserved marinade.
Remove roast from oven and let stand for 15 minutes. Combine pan drippings with remaining marinade. Bring to a boil, reduce heat and simmer for 1 minute. Serve with roast.

Oriental Short Ribs

4 SERVINGS

3 pounds beef short ribs
Flour, for dredging
2 tablespoons vegetable oil
½ cup teriyaki sauce
1 garlic clove, crushed
½ teaspoon ginger
⅛ teaspoon cloves
1¼ cups water
¼ cup flour
½ cup water

Dredge ribs in flour. Heat oil in Dutch oven and brown ribs thoroughly. Drain excess oil from meat.
Combine remaining ingredients except flour and water, and pour over ribs. Simmer, covered, for 2 hours or until meat is tender.
Combine flour and water, whisking to a smooth paste.
Remove ribs from Dutch oven to a warm platter.
Pour pan drippings into a large measuring cup, skim off fat. Add enough water to measure 2½ cups, return to Dutch oven.
Gradually stir in flour and water mixture, simmering until mixture thickens.
Serve thickened pan juices with ribs.

Curried Tomato Beef

4 SERVINGS

1½ pounds flank steak, cut in strips
2 tablespoons cornstarch
1 tablespoon water
3 tablespoons soy sauce
3 tablespoons vegetable oil
1 medium onion, chopped
1 green pepper, seeded and julienned
1 tablespoon brown sugar
1 tablespoon curry powder
1 28-ounce can tomatoes

Marinate flank steak strips in cornstarch, water and soy sauce for 15 minutes, tossing every few minutes.
Heat wok and add 1 tablespoon oil. Stir-fry onion and green pepper about 1 minute. Push aside.
Add 2 tablespoons oil to wok and add strips of flank steak. Mix brown sugar, 1 tablespoon soy sauce and curry powder and drizzle over meat. Stir-fry meat just until pink color disappears.
Stir in onions and peppers and tomatoes. Mix well and heat through.
Serve over rice or noodles.

Pork Rolls

6 SERVINGS

1 pound lean ground pork
¼ teaspoon pepper
1½ teaspoons garlic powder
1 teaspoon salt
1 egg, beaten
1 tablespoon parsley
1 cup soft bread crumbs
1 cup flour
1 teaspoon olive oil

Mix together pork, pepper, garlic powder, salt, egg, and parsley. Add bread crumbs and lightly mix until mixture binds together. Form into 6 small rolls. Dredge rolls in flour. Heat olive oil in a heavy skillet and sauté rolls until golden brown and thoroughly cooked. Drain and serve warm.

Glazed Pot Roast

8 SERVINGS

1 tablespoon butter
3 to 4 pound beef pot roast
1 teaspoon salt
¼ teaspoon pepper
1 10½-ounce can cream of celery soup
½ cup onion rings
1 8-ounce package cream cheese
1 teaspoon prepared horseradish
Gravy:
¼ cup water
2 to 3 tablespoons flour
2 cups pan drippings

Pre-heat oven to 325°F.
Melt butter in Dutch oven. Season meat with salt and pepper. Brown meat slowly on both sides.
Spread soup over top of roast, add onions. Cover and roast for 2½ to 3 hours, or until roast is tender.
Pour off 2 cups pan drippings and set aside.
Blend cream cheese and horseradish and spread on top of roast. Return to oven, uncovered and heat 3 to 5 minutes to glaze.
To make gravy, whisk water and flour together to make a smooth paste. Heat pan drippings to boiling. Stir flour and water paste into drippings, stirring constantly. Simmer for 3 minutes, or until thickened.
Serve gravy with roast.

Winter in the Country—A Cold Morning

Pork Fillets

6 SERVINGS

1 6-pound pork tenderloin
1 cup soy sauce
5 cups red wine or water
l large onion, sliced
1 garlic clove, crushed
12 peppercorns, crushed
1 medium carrot, sliced
4 tablespoons fresh ginger, grated
4 tablespoons butter
2 tablespoons flour
2 tablespoons Dijon mustard

Slice the pork into 12 equal strips, place in a large bowl and refrigerate while preparing marinade.

Combine the soy sauce and wine or water in a large saucepan. Add onion, garlic, peppercorns, carrot and ginger. Bring to a boil and simmer for 20 minutes.

Pour the marinade over the pork strips. Marinate for 8 hours, turning occasionally.

Pre-heat oven to 350°F.

Remove the pork from the marinade and dry. Place pork between sheets of waxed paper and pound flat. Melt 2 tablespoons of butter in a heavy skillet and sauté the pork briefly. Transfer the pork to an oven-proof casserole. Add enough marinade to cover the meat, reserving the remainder. Bake for 1½ hours.

Remove pork to a heated serving platter. Melt the remaining butter in a saucepan. Whisk in the flour and reserved marinade. Stir constantly over low heat until the mixture thickens. Stir in the mustard and simmer for 15 minutes, stirring occasionally.

To serve, strain thickened marinade mixture and serve over pork.

Central Park in Winter

Sausage-Pepper Skillet

6 SERVINGS

1 pound sausage, cut into 1-inch pieces
2 medium onions, sliced
1 tablespoon vegetable oil
1 13¼-ounce can beef broth
1 cup long-grain rice
1 medium green pepper, seeded and julienned
1 medium tomato, coarsely chopped

Cook sausage and onions in vegetable oil in a heavy skillet over medium heat until sausage is browned. Drain excess fat from skillet.

Add enough water to broth to make 2½ cups liquid. Add broth liquid and rice to skillet and bring to a boil. Stir in green pepper and tomatoes. Cover tightly and simmer 20 minutes.

Remove from heat. Let stand, covered, until liquid is absorbed, about 5 minutes.

Lamb Chops

4 SERVINGS

¼ cup butter, softened
2 tablespoons molasses
1 tablespoon cider vinegar
2 tablespoons onion, minced
½ teaspoon salt
⅛ teaspoon pepper
¼ teaspoon ginger
¼ teaspoon dry mustard
4 lamb chops

Mix together all ingredients except lamb chops. Brush chops generously with sauce and marinate 1 hour.

Pre-heat broiler.

Broil lamb chops to desired doneness, basting frequently with sauce.

Serve with remaining sauce.

POULTRY

Red Chicken Cacciatore

2 SERVINGS

2 chicken breast halves
2 tablespoons flour
Salt and pepper, to taste
2 tablespoons olive oil
1 small yellow onion, sliced
1 small green pepper, seeded and thinly sliced
1 small carrot, peeled and thinly sliced
1 small rib celery, diced
1 garlic clove, crushed
1 14 ½-ounce can tomatoes

Sprinkle chicken with flour, salt and pepper. Heat oil in a 10-inch heavy skillet over medium-high heat until almost smoking. Place chicken in skillet and quickly brown for 6 to 8 minutes, turning twice. Grease will splatter, so use a grease splatter screen or partially cover pan.

Push chicken to side of pan, and add onion, green pepper, carrot and celery. Simmer, stirring often, until onion is transparent. Stir in garlic and simmer 1 minute longer. Stir in tomatoes, bring mixture back to a simmer. Pull chicken away from sides of pan and spoon mixture over chicken. Reduce heat to low and cook, covered, for 20 minutes.

Hot Chicken Salad

6 SERVINGS

4 cups cooked chicken, cubed
4 cups celery, finely chopped
2 teaspoons salt
½ teaspoon tarragon
¼ cup grated onion
1 tablespoon lemon juice
2 cups mayonnaise
¼ cup dry white wine or water
1 cup almonds, toasted and slivered
1 cup bread crumbs
½ cup Parmesan cheese

Thoroughly combine chicken, celery, salt, tarragon, onion, lemon juice, mayonnaise, wine or water and almonds. Allow to stand 1 hour.

Spoon mixture into a greased 8 × 12-inch baking pan. Top with bread crumbs and Parmesan cheese. Bake in a 350°F oven for 25 to 30 minutes, or until heated through and lightly browned.

Mexican Turkey Bake

6 SERVINGS

1 cup rice
1 3-ounce can mild green chilies, drained and chopped
3 cups cooked turkey, cubed
1 12-ounce can Mexican-style corn with peppers, drained
1 10-ounce can enchilada sauce
¾ teaspoon salt
1 cup sour cream

Pre-heat oven to 350°F.

Prepare rice according to package directions. Place in a large mixing bowl.

Reserve 1 tablespoon chilies for garnish, combine remaining chilies, turkey, corn, enchilada sauce, and salt with rice. Mix well.

Spoon mixture into a greased 12 × 7 ½ × 2-inch casserole. Cover and bake about 25 minutes, until casserole is hot.

To serve, spoon sour cream down center of casserole and garnish with reserved chilies.

Cajun Chicken

4 to 6 SERVINGS

3-pound chicken, cut up
3 tablespoons vegetable oil
1 medium onion, coarsely chopped
1 medium green pepper, chopped
1 garlic clove, minced
1 28-ounce whole tomatoes, quartered
⅓ cup soy sauce
¼ teaspoon cayenne
1 10-ounce package frozen okra, thawed and drained

Brown chicken pieces on all sides in hot oil in Dutch oven medium heat. Remove and set aside.

Add onion, green pepper and garlic to skillet and sauté until onion is transparent.

Stir in tomatoes, soy sauce, and cayenne and bring to a boil. Arrange chicken pieces in sauce and cover skillet. Simmer over low heat for 50 minutes, turning chicken once.

Stir in okra and simmer, covered for 10 minutes longer, or until okra is tender.

Serve chicken and sauce over hot rice.

Turkey Chili with Rice

6 SERVINGS

1 pound ground turkey
3 cups chicken broth
1 16-ounce can tomatoes, chopped
1 6-ounce can tomato paste
1 cup long-grain rice
2 ribs celery, chopped
1 small onion, chopped
1 small green pepper, seeded and chopped
1 garlic clove, minced
2 to 4 teaspoons chili powder, or more, to taste

Spread turkey in a shallow layer in a non-stick skillet and cook over medium heat until underside is brown. Break turkey into chunks and brown on all sides. Add remaining ingredients. Cover and simmer, stirring occasionally, about 25 minutes or until rice is tender.

Easy Chicken Cacciatore

4 SERVINGS

2 medium onions, sliced
2 garlic cloves, minced
2 tablespoons olive oil
1 2 1/2-3 pound chicken, cut up
1 16-ounce can stewed tomatoes
1 8-ounce can tomato sauce
1/2 pound small mushrooms, cleaned

1/2 teaspoon salt
1/4 teaspoon pepper
2 teaspoons Italian seasoning
1/4 cup dry white wine or water
Hot cooked rice to serve 4

Sauté onions and garlic in a large skillet over medium heat until onions are transparent. Remove onions and set aside.
Brown chicken in same skillet over medium heat, turning to brown for 15 minutes. Add more oil if needed.
Return onions to skillet. Combine undrained tomatoes, tomato sauce, mushrooms, salt, pepper and Italian seasoning. Pour over chicken in skillet, cover and simmer for 30 minutes.
Stir in wine or water. Cook, uncovered, over low heat 10-15 minutes longer or until chicken is tender, turning occasionally.
Place cooked rice on serving platter and serve chicken and mixture over rice.

Chicken Marengo with Brown Rice

6 SERVINGS

1 cup brown rice
1 fryer, cut up
2 tablespoons vegetable oil
1 16-ounce can stewed tomatoes
2 medium onions, cut in wedges
1 tablespoon cornstarch
1/4 cup white wine or water

Prepare rice according to package directions. While rice is cooking, brown chicken in oil in a 12-inch skillet over medium heat, about 10 minutes each side. Drain off fat. Add tomatoes and onions. Cover and simmer until chicken is tender, about 20 minutes. Remove chicken and keep warm.
Combine cornstarch and wine or water. Stir into tomato mixture in skillet and bring to a boil. Cook, stirring constantly, until sauce thickens, about 2 minutes. Spoon cooked rice onto serving platter and top with chicken and sauce.

Chicken Stir-Fry with Noodles

4 SERVINGS

1 whole chicken breast, skinned and boned
5 tablespoons cornstarch
5 tablespoons teriyaki sauce
1 garlic clove, minced
2 teaspoons catsup
1 cup water
2 cups uncooked fine egg noodles
2 tablespoons vegetable oil
1 medium onion, chopped

Cut chicken in 1/2-inch square pieces. Mix cornstarch with 1 tablespoon teriyaki sauce and garlic. Stir in chicken and marinate for 30 minutes.
Mix remaining cornstarch, teriyaki sauce, catsup and water. Set aside.
Cook noodles according to directions and keep warm on a serving platter.
Heat 1 tablespoon oil in a heated wok or large skillet over high heat. Add chicken and stir-fry 2 minutes and remove.
Heat remaining oil in same wok or skillet. Add onion and stir-fry until onion is transparent. Add chicken and teriyaki sauce mixture to onion. Cook, stirring constantly, until mixture thickens.
Pour over hot noodles and toss to combine to serve.

Chicken with Apricot Curry

4 SERVINGS

3 medium chicken breast halves, skinned and boned
2½ tablespoons flour
½ teaspoon paprika
1 teaspoon salt
Pepper, to taste
1 small green pepper, julienned
1 medium onion, sliced
1 cup unsweetened pineapple juice
1 teaspoon granulated chicken bouillon
1 garlic clove, crushed
¾ teaspoon curry powder
1 bay leaf
1 16-ounce can apricot halves

Pre-heat oven to 350°F.

Cut chicken breasts into chunks. Place chicken in oven-proof casserole with lid. Mix together flour, paprika, salt and pepper and sprinkle over chicken. Toss chicken to coat with mixture.

Sprinkle the pepper strips and sliced onion on top of chicken chunks, toss lightly and set aside.

In a small bowl, mix pineapple juice, bouillon, garlic, curry powder, and bay leaf. Set aside.

Drain liquid from apricots. Place apricot halves, cut side down on top of vegetable-chicken mixture in the casserole. Pour the pineapple juice mixture over the casserole.

Cover and bake for 40 minutes. Uncover and baste with liquid in casserole and continue baking for an additional 15-20 minutes.

To serve, remove bay leaf and serve with steamed rice.

Duck Stuffed with Apricots

6 SERVINGS

1 roasting duck, 4 to 5 pounds
1 pound fresh apricots, seeded
1 orange
1 onion, finely chopped
2 tablespoons oil
3 tablespoons honey
1 to 1½ cups stock made with duck giblets (or one
*   chicken bouillon cube dissolved in 1 to 1½ cups*
*   water)*
3 to 4 tablespoons apricot brandy

Pre-heat oven to 400°F.

Stuff duck with half the seeded apricots, 3 strips of orange zest (keep remainder of orange for juice), onion, and season to taste. Prick skin of duck with fork to allow fat to run out while cooking.

Heat oil in roasting pan. When hot, add duck and baste with oil. Roast in oven, allowing 20 minutes per pound. Thirty minutes before cooking is completed, spoon melted honey and juice of orange over skin. Ten minutes before end of cooking, add remainder of apricots to pan; roast until warm and slightly browned. Place duck on a warm platter, and remove stuffing to a separate bowl. Arrange roasted apricots around duck.

Pour duck fat, stock, and stuffing into a saucepan and bring to a boil, stirring constantly. When the sauce has a pleasant flavor, place in blender and blend until smooth. Return to heat and add apricot brandy.

Serve at once with duck and apricots.

Duck Stuffed with Apricots

Dutch Apple Cake

DESSERTS

Dutch Apple Cake

MAKES 1 8-INCH CAKE

1¹/₃ cups cake flour
¹/₂ teaspoon salt
1 teaspoon baking powder
³/₄ cup margarine
³/₄ cup sugar
2 egg yolks
3 tablespoons milk
1 pound tart apples, peeled, cored, and sliced
1 teaspoon ground cinnamon

Pre-heat oven to 375°F. Grease an 8-inch square cake pan.

Reserve 2 tablespoons of the flour; sift the rest with the salt and baking powder.

Cream ½ cup of margarine with 1 tablespoon of sugar. Add egg yolks and milk, and beat until light and fluffy. Blend in flour mixture, and stir until smooth. Spread batter in the cake pan. Arrange apples on top. Combine the reserved 2 tablespoons of flour with the remaining margarine, sugar, and cinnamon. Mix with fork until mixture is crumbly. Sprinkle over apples, and bake for 45 minutes or until well-browned.

Nut Bread

2 9 × 5 × 3-INCH LOAVES

⅔ cup shortening
2⅔ cups sugar
4 eggs
⅔ cup water
3⅓ cups flour
2 teaspoons baking soda
1 teaspoon cinnamon
1 teaspoon salt
½ teaspoon ground cloves
½ teaspoon nutmeg
1 cup walnuts or pecans, chopped

Pre-heat oven to 350°F. Grease 2 9 × 5 × 3-inch loaf pans.

Cream shortening and sugar. Add eggs, one at a time, beating well after each addition. Stir in water.

Combine flour, baking soda, cinnamon, salt, cloves and nutmeg. Beat into shortening mixture for 1 minute, scraping bowl frequently. Stir in nuts.

Pour into greased loaf pans. Bake 60 to 70 minutes, or until a toothpick inserted in center of each loaf comes out clean.

Cook pans on wire rack 10 minutes. Remove bread from pans, and cool completely.

Date Cookies

5 DOZEN COOKIES

1 cup butter
2 cups brown sugar, firmly packed
2 eggs
3½ cups flour
1 teaspoon baking soda
1 teaspoon salt
1 cup plain yogurt
1 cup dates, chopped
1 egg white, lightly beaten
Sugar, for sprinkling

Pre-heat oven to 400°F.

Cream together butter, sugar and eggs. Sift flour, baking soda and salt together. Stir in sifted dry ingredients alternately with yogurt.

Mix in chopped dates. Drop by teaspoonsful onto greased baking sheets. Brush with beaten egg white and sprinkle with sugar.

Bake 8 to 10 minutes or until lightly browned. Cook on wire racks.

Apple Cherry Muffins

12 MUFFINS

2 cups flour, sifted
½ cup sugar
1 tablespoon baking powder
½ teaspoon salt
1 teaspoon cinnamon
1 egg
¾ cup milk
¼ cup butter, melted
¾ cup apple, pared and finely chopped
½ cup maraschino cherries

Pre-heat oven to 400°F.

Grease 12 muffin cups and line with paper cups, if desired.

Sift together flour, sugar, baking powder, salt and cinnamon. Beat together egg and milk. Stir in butter. Add to dry ingredients, mixing just enough to moisten. Fold in chopped apple and cherries.

Fill greased muffin cups two-thirds full. Bake for 20 to 25 minutes.

Mud Cake

1 9 × 13-INCH CAKE

Cake:
4 eggs
2 cups sugar
1 cup butter, melted
2 teaspoons baking powder
⅓ cup cocoa
1 teaspoon vanilla
1 cup pecans, chopped
1 17-ounce jar marshmallow creme
Frosting:
½ cup butter, melted
6 tablespoons milk
⅓ cup cocoa
1 teaspoon vanilla
1 1-pound box confectioner's sugar
¾ cup pecans, chopped

Pre-heat oven to 350°F.

Beat eggs with sugar. Add remaining cake ingredients, except marshmallow creme and mix well. Pour into a greased and floured 9 × 13-inch pan.

Bake cake for 30 minutes. Do not overbake. Remove cake from oven and spread with marshmallow creme while still hot.

Mix frosting ingredients, beating well and spread over cooled cake.

Hot Chocolate Soufflé

6 SERVINGS

2 tablespoons butter
3 level tablespoons flour
¾ cup milk
4 squares dark sweet chocolate
½ square bitter chocolate
5 tablespoons sugar
2 tablespoons rum
5 egg yolks
5 egg whites, stiffly beaten
Sauce:
1 egg
2 tablespoons red wine
Confectioner's sugar, to garnish

Pre-heat oven to 375°F.
Melt butter in small heavy pan and stir in flour until smooth. Add milk slowly, stirring constantly, until mixture thickens. Do not allow to boil.
Melt chocolate in double boiler. Stir in sugar and rum. Combine with milk mixture.
Beat egg yolks together, and stir into milk mixture. Fold in stiffly beaten egg whites.
Tie a band of greased waxed paper around a greased soufflé dish. Dust inside of dish with granulated sugar. Pour in soufflé mixture. Place in pan of hot water and bake for 45 minutes.
10 minutes before baking time ends, combine sauce ingredients in top of double boiler over low heat. Beat with rotary beater until thick.
After soufflé bakes, carefully remove paper and dust soufflé with confectioners' sugar.
Serve soufflé at once, with sauce on the side.

Pecan Spice Cake

1 8-INCH SQUARE

2 cups flour
1 teaspoon baking powder
½ teaspoon baking soda
¾ teaspoon salt
1 teaspoon cinnamon
½ teaspoon mace
1½ teaspoons ground cloves
½ cup butter
1 cup sugar
3 eggs
½ cup chopped pecans
¼ cup molasses
1 cup milk

Pre-heat oven to 350°F. Grease a square 8-inch baking pan.
Sift flour, baking powder, baking soda, salt and spices together.
Cream butter until soft. Gradually beat in sugar. Add eggs and beat well. Stir in chopped pecans. Stir the molasses and milk together. Add the flour mixture alternately with the molasses mixture, beating well after each addition.
Pour batter into prepared pan and bake for 40 to 50 minutes.

Honey Cake

2 8-INCH LAYERS

Cake batter:
3 squares unsweetened baking chocolate
8 tablespoons honey
1½ cups cake flour
1 teaspoon baking soda
½ teaspoon salt
½ cup butter
¼ cup sugar
1 teaspoon vanilla
2 eggs
½ cup water
Frosting:
6 squares unsweetened baking chocolate
4 tablespoons honey
1½ cups confectioner's sugar
2 tablespoons warm water

Pre-heat oven to 350°F. Grease two 8-inch round cake pans and dust with flour.
To make the cake, melt unsweetened chocolate and honey in the top of a double boiler. Cool, then beat for 3 minutes.
Sift flour, baking soda and salt together.
Cream butter and sugar until light and fluffy. Beat in chocolate mixture and vanilla. Beat in eggs, one at a time. Add flour mixture alternately with water, beating well after each addition.
Pour into cake pans and bake for 45 minutes. Cool in pans for 10 minutes. Remove from pans and cool before frosting.
To make frosting, melt honey and unsweetened chocolate in the top of a double boiler. Remove from heat and beat in half the confectioner's sugar. Stir in water and remaining confectioner's sugar. Fill and frost the cooled cake.

Chocolate Balls

APPROXIMATELY 40 SMALL COOKIES

3 squares unsweetened baking chocolate
1 tablespoon strong black coffee
1 cup butter or margarine
¼ cup sugar
1 egg yolk
1 cup chopped walnuts or pecans
1 tablespoon rum
2½ cups flour, sifted
Sugar, to roll

Pre-heat oven to 350°F.

Break up chocolate into small pieces and put into a double boiler with the coffee. Stir until melted. Let cool.

Cream butter and sugar together until light and fluffy. Beat in egg yolk. Add nuts and rum. Stir in cooled chocolate. Add sifted flour and blend to a smooth dough. Wrap in foil and chill for 1 hour.

Form teaspoons of the dough into balls, roll well in sugar, and arrange on greased baking sheets, leaving space between balls. Press half a nut into each ball and bake for approximately 15 minutes.

Chocolate Balls

Marbled Chocolate Loaf

Marbled Chocolate Loaf

1 9½ × 5 × 3–INCH CAKE

¹/₃ cup shortening
1 cup sugar
1 teaspoon vanilla extract
2 cups cake flour
2¹/₂ teaspoons baking powder
¹/₄ teaspoon salt
²/₃ cup milk
3 egg whites
1 square baking chocolate, melted
2 tablespoons hot water
¹/₄ teaspoon baking soda

Pre-heat oven to 350°F.

Beat shortening and sugar until light and fluffy. Add vanilla. Sift together flour, baking powder, and salt, and add to creamed mixture alternately with milk. Beat well with each addition. Beat egg whites stiffly and fold into mixture.

Mix melted chocolate with water and baking soda. Add this mixture to half the cake batter.

Alternate light and dark batters by spoonfuls in a greased, lined loaf pan approximately 9½ by 5 by 3 inches. Bake for 40 to 45 minutes.

When cold, frost with chocolate icing.